# Conquering Interviews for Business Roles in Tech

## Getting Job Offers in Strategy, Operations, Product, Marketing, and More

Daniel Li

*To my parents,*
*for supporting and inspiring me.*

# Table of Contents

# Introduction

## What is the goal of this book?

The goal of this book is to prepare students and working professionals for interviewing for business roles in tech companies.

These interviews cover a wide range of questions. Types of questions you may get asked include:

- Company research questions

- Behavioral & resume questions

- Motivational questions

- Case interviews

- Mini-cases

- Data challenges

This book will provide you with efficient and effective strategies for dealing with all of these different types of interview questions.

This book focuses on non-technical business roles in technology companies. The strategies and practice questions in this book are helpful for those interviewing for roles in:

- Strategy & business operations

- Product management

- Product marketing

- Business development

- Corporate development

- Operations

- Analytics

- Finance

Also, this book will provide a wide range of practice questions from all major technology sectors. These sectors include:

- E-commerce

- Internet

- Software

- Hardware

- Telecom

By the end of the book, you will be familiar with all of these sectors.

Finally, the strategies and practice questions in this book apply to technology companies of any size or stage, from early-stage startups to large tech companies.

Regardless of which tech sector, role, or company that you are interviewing for, this book will provide fundamental strategies to help you land your dream job offer.

## How is this book organized?

I have organized this book by the six different categories of interview questions:

- Company research questions

- Behavioral & resume questions

- Motivational questions

- Case interviews

- Mini-cases

    o Strategy & business operations questions

    o Product management & marketing questions

    o Business & corporate development questions

    o Operations questions

    o Analytics questions

    o Finance questions

- Data challenges

For each type of question, we'll understand what interviewers are looking for, learn the most effective strategies, and practice with real interview questions from a wide range of companies.

There are many supplementary handouts and templates that come with this book. You can access all of these files by sending an email to **conquer.interviews@gmail.com** with the subject "**Get More**". An automated email will send you everything.

If you are ready, feel free to move onto the next chapter to begin learning how to prepare for interviews for business roles in tech.

For the remainder of this chapter, I'll provide a concise introduction to tech and the different types of roles. This may be helpful for those who are new or unfamiliar with the tech industry.

# What are tech companies?

Technology is the collection of techniques, skills, and processes used to produce goods, services, or to achieve an objective.

Tech companies are businesses that focus on the development and manufacturing of technology. They can also be businesses that are dependent on technology for their primary source of revenue.

There are five major sectors in technology.

**E-commerce**: Companies that engage in or facilitate the buying and selling of goods and services using the internet. Examples include Alibaba, Amazon, eBay, Etsy, Flipkart, Groupon, PayPal, Rakuten, Shopify, Square, Tencent, and Wayfair.

**Internet**: Companies that conduct their business primarily on the internet, having a business model that would be impossible without the internet. Examples include Airbnb, Amazon, Baidu, Facebook, Google, LinkedIn, Netflix, Twitter, Uber, and Yahoo.

**Software**: Companies that develop and distribute software. Examples include Adobe, Box, Dropbox, Intuit, Oracle, Salesforce, SAP, Slack, Workday, and VMware.

**Hardware**: Companies that build and sell hardware. Examples include Apple, HP, IBM, Huawei, Intel, Microsoft, Nintendo, Lenovo, Qualcomm, Samsung, and Sony.

**Telecom**: Companies that provide the infrastructure to make communication possible, connecting people and things together. Examples include AT&T, China Mobile, Deutsche Telekom, T-Mobile, Verizon, and Vodafone.

Some companies can fall into multiple sectors. As technology continues to advance, the distinctions among these sectors become less apparent.

# Why work in tech?

There are many compelling reasons why people want to work in tech companies.

**High pay**: The tech industry is one of the highest paying industries. Tech companies compensate their employees well.

**Office perks and benefits**: In addition to high pay, many tech companies offer extraordinary perks and benefits. These include catered meals, fully-stocked snack pantries, childcare, and on-site gym and recreation.

**Work-life balance**: Tech companies have an outstanding work-life balance. It is not uncommon to work fewer than forty hours a week at large tech companies. Startups have longer working hours, but you will still be working far fewer hours compared to consulting and finance.

**Challenging work**: Tech companies face challenging problems in how to innovate, grow, and outcompete competitors. By working in tech, you'll be at the forefront of solving these challenges.

**Interest in technology**: Many people that work in tech have a strong passion for technology. They are interested in the latest innovations and advancements in technology.

For these reasons, employment in tech has proliferated over the past years. It is an attractive and highly desirable industry to work in.

# What are the different types of roles?

While there are hundreds of different business roles at tech companies, there are eight major categories.

**Strategy & business operations**: These roles set and drive key business initiatives. Examples of titles include:

- Business Strategy & Operations

- Corporate Strategy

- Strategic Planning & Analysis

- Strategy Manager

- Business Operations

**Product management**: These roles create and execute a roadmap for product features and requirements. Examples of titles include:

- Product Manager

- Product Operations

- Category Manager

**Product marketing**: These roles bring a product to market by identifying customer segments and needs, developing the right marketing messages, and identifying the proper channels to launch in. Examples of titles include:

- Product Marketing Manager

- Marketing Manager

**Business development**: These roles identify new partners, expand relationships with existing partners, and negotiate deals and contracts. Examples of titles include:

- Business Development

- Corporate Strategy

- Strategic Partnerships

- Partnership Sales

**Corporate development**: These roles identify potential acquisitions and investments, oversee the due diligence process, and manage the execution of the deals. Examples of titles include:

- Corporate Development

- Corporate Strategy

**Operations**: These roles support procurement, manufacturing, fulfillment, and other logistics. Examples of titles include:

- Worldwide Operations

- Sales Operations

- Operations Manager

**Analytics**: These roles conduct data analysis to generate insights to make predictions and business decisions. Examples of titles include:

- Data Scientist

- Business Analyst

- People Analytics

**Finance**: These roles support financing, capital structuring, and investment decisions. Examples of titles include:

- Financial Planning & Analysis

- Corporate Finance

The strategies in this book will help you prepare for interviews at any of these roles.

## What are the different stages of tech companies?

Tech companies are segmented into four distinct categories based on their stage.

**Early-stage startups**: These are startups that have yet to raise Series A fundraising. These startups are focused on building their product, deploying their product with early customers, and demonstrating product-market fit.

Startups in this stage have taken on many risks, including product risk, engineering risk, market risk, team risk, and execution risk. However, working at these startups has the highest potential compensation upside.

What to expect working at an early-stage startup:

- High amounts of equity

- Long working hours

- Unstable and risky employment

- High level of autonomy and responsibility

- Opportunity to work across all functions

- Constantly changing roles and responsibilities

- Ambiguous and unstructured problems

- Flat organizational structure with minimal layers

**Series A startups**: These are startups that have completed their Series A fundraising. These companies have proved their product-market fit and are focused on scaling rapidly and predictably. Series A startups are still risky to work for. However, compared to early-stage startups, Series A startups have more defined roles.

**Growth stage startups**: These are companies that have raised Series B, C, D, and beyond. Growth stage startups have already determined the best way to scale and have set up the resources and infrastructure needed to make it happen. These startups are focused on continuing to grow rapidly and sustainably.

Working at these startups is much less risky than working at early-stage and Series A startups. Growth stage startups have even more clearly defined roles and responsibilities and shorter working hours, but have much lower compensation upside from equity.

**Mature technology companies**: These are companies that have gone through an initial public offering (IPO) or are close to going through one. These companies have been around for many years.

At this stage, most of the rapid growth for the company has slowed down. The company is now focused on maintaining and defending their market share while looking for adjacent markets to grow into.

What to expect working at a mature technology company:

- Significantly less equity, but more guaranteed compensation

- Stable working hours

- Stable job employment

- Clearly defined roles and responsibilities

- Organizational structure with many layers

# What does the interview process look like?

Interviews for business roles in tech vary significantly depending on both the company and the role. There is no single interview process that all tech companies follow.

However, below are a few examples of the interview process at different companies to give you an idea of what you could expect.

**Airbnb**: Strategic Planning & Analysis

1.  A 30-minute informal chat with a team member to ask questions

2.  A 30-minute interview with the hiring manager focused on behavioral questions and mini-cases

3.  A data challenge take-home assignment

4.  Two 40-minute interviews with team members focused on mini-cases

5.  A 30-minute interview with the team lead focused on behavioral and motivational questions

**Series B Startup**: Business Operations

1.  A 30-minute interview with the recruiter focused on motivational questions

2.  A 45-minute interview with the hiring manager focused on resume questions, behavioral questions, and mini-cases

3.  Three 45-minute interviews focused on motivational questions and mini-cases

**LinkedIn**: Product Marketing Manager

1.  A 30-minute interview with the recruiter focused on motivational questions

2. A 45-minute interview with the hiring manager focused on behavioral questions and mini-cases

3. A data challenge take-home assignment

4. A 1-hour presentation on the data challenge assignment and two 30-minute interviews focused on behavioral questions

**Netflix**: Content Marketing Strategy

1. A 30-minute interview with the recruiter focused on behavioral questions

2. A 1-hour interview with the hiring manager focused on case interviews

3. Five 30-minute interviews focused on mini-cases and behavioral questions

Regardless of what the interview process looks like, you can prepare for any interview by preparing for all of the different types of questions you could get asked.

# Conducting Company Research

## Why do you need to do company research?

There are two main reasons why you should thoroughly research the company that you are interviewing for.

One, knowing the company well demonstrates your interest in the company or role. If you show up to an interview without any understanding of what the company does, interviewers will assume that you are not interested or serious about the role.

Two, thoroughly researching the company allows you to speak intelligently when asked interview questions. For case interviews and mini-cases, having background knowledge of the company can help significantly improve your answer.

By thoroughly researching the company, you will stand out from candidates who only have basic knowledge.

This does not mean that you need to research every fact about the company. You can easily spend hundreds of hours reading press releases, analyst reports, and tech articles. Instead, be smart in your research and focus on learning the most important things.

In this chapter, we'll walk through the essential information you need to know when conducting company research.

## Where do I do company research?

There are four different sources of information you should consider when conducting company research.

**10-K Annual Report**: All public companies are required to file an annual report on its financial performance called the 10-K. You can find this document under "Investor Relations" on company websites or the SEC government website.

The 10-K is a fairly comprehensive document and is a fantastic first starting point to learn about the company. Useful information you'll find in a 10-K include:

- Company products and services

- Company financial performance

- Major competitors

- Recent significant events

- Risks to the business

If the company is private and does not have a 10-K, they may still publish some kind of annual report for their investors that you can look at.

**Tech articles**: The second source of information are tech articles written by various media companies. I highly recommend reading TechCrunch, but other sources include The Verge, Gizmodo, Engadget, and Axios.

Tech articles provide news and perspectives on tech companies from an outsider or third-party perspective. In contrast, the 10-K is a report that comes from the company itself. Therefore, the information in tech articles will be much more subjective.

In tech articles, you'll find useful information on companies such as:

- Recent significant events

- Perspectives on how these events impact customers, competitors, and the company's future

- Viewpoints on how well the company is performing

- Opinions on what the company should be doing differently

Reading tech articles will help you develop a perspective or viewpoint on the company beyond the objective information that the 10-K provides.

**Current and former employees**: Speak to at least one person that is a current or former employee of the company that you are interviewing for. Preferably, speak to someone that currently or previously worked in the exact role you are interviewing for.

This will give you information on:

- The culture of the company

- Skills or attributes the company values

- The fit of the role within the broader organization

- The responsibilities and tasks of the role

- Working styles of people on the team

You will likely not find much information on these topics online, so use your network to find a current or former employee to speak to.

**Analyst reports**: These reports are written by financial analysts to provide investment guidance to investors.

Analyst reports are found through online platforms such as Thomson Reuters, Morningstar, Standard & Poor's Capital IQ, and Argus. However, you will need a subscription to these services.

You can find less detailed summaries of analyst reports through summary sites, such as Yahoo Finance, Reuters, Zacks Investment Research, and NASDAQ.com.

There are three types of analyst reports:

- Initiating coverage reports are released when a firm starts covering a company for the first time. They provide information on company history, trends, and competitors

- Company analyst reports focus on the financial performance of the company, but also have some qualitative analysis

- Industry analyst reports have detailed analysis of an entire industry. They provide information on market sizes, shares, and major trends

# What do I need to know?

We can categorize all of the information you need to know into objective and subjective information.

Objective information is based on factual evidence. It does not require you to take a stance or have an opinion because this type of information is generally accepted to be true.

There are seven objective pieces of information you need to know:

- What markets does the company play in?

- What is their mission statement or aspiration?

- What are their products and services and what percentage of total revenue do they make up?

- Who are their customers?

- What is their business model?

- Who are their competitors?

- What are the significant events that have happened at the company over the past few years?

The company's 10-K or other annual reports will have nearly all of this information.

Next, research subjective information, which is writing based on personal opinions, interpretations, and judgment. Subjective information can be found in tech articles and analyst reports.

The goal is to build a perspective of the company. You should have an opinion on how the company is doing, what they should be focusing on, and what their challenges are.

A SWOT analysis is a helpful framework for conducting your subjective research. SWOT stands for strengths, weaknesses, opportunities, and threats.

There are four essential things you should have a perspective on:

- **Strengths**: What do they do well? What qualities separate them from competitors?

- **Weaknesses**: What do they do poorly? What are the things that competitors do better?

- **Opportunities**: Where are the opportunities for growth or improvement?

- **Threats**: Who are the most threatening competitors? What are the major risks to the company's business?

If you can answer these questions, you will have a solid foundational perspective on the company.

In addition to researching the company, you should also investigate the specific role and team you are interviewing for. Speaking to current and former employees will be the most helpful for this.

There are five essential questions you should know:

- What are the responsibilities or tasks of the role?

- What skills or attributes are preferred or required?

- How does the role fit with the broader organization?

- What are the primary goals or targets of the team?

- What is the culture of the team and company like?

You can access a comprehensive template for conducting company research by emailing **conquer.interviews@gmail.com** with the subject "**Get More**". An automated email will send you all supplementary information that comes with this book.

## Example of company research

Let's take a look at an example of what completed company research looks like. We'll research the company LinkedIn for an upcoming product marketing interview.

*LinkedIn Company Research*

*What markets does the company play in?*

- *Social media*

- *Job search and recruiting*

- *Advertising*

- *Online learning*

*What is their mission statement or aspiration?*

- *To connect the world's professionals to make them more productive and successful*

*What are their products and services and what percentage of total revenue do they make up?*

- *LinkedIn is a professional network that is free to join and use*

- *However, LinkedIn has three main offerings that generate revenue: Talent Solutions, Marketing Solutions, and Premium subscriptions*

- *Talent Solutions represents ~65% of LinkedIn's revenue and consists of two parts. The first part helps recruiters attract, recruit, and hire talent. The second part, Learning Solutions, offers online courses to enterprise clients and individuals*

- *Marketing Solutions represents ~18% of LinkedIn's revenue. LinkedIn sells advertising and sponsored postings*

- *Premium subscriptions represent ~17% of LinkedIn's revenue. This offering allows users to increase their search results, send messages, contact members outside of their networks, and see information about people that have viewed their profile*

- *Premium subscriptions also include Sales Solutions, which enables users to generate quality leads to increase sales*

*Who are their customers?*

- *LinkedIn's free users are primarily working professionals*

- *For Talent Solutions, customers are recruiters and other human resources employees*

- *For Marketing Solutions, customers are advertising, marketing, and sales employees*

- *For Premium subscriptions, customers are job seekers, recruiters, and salespeople*

*What is their business model?*

- *LinkedIn operates a freemium business model*

- *LinkedIn attracts a large user base by making it free for anyone to join and use*

- *LinkedIn then makes money by selling premium offerings to a subset of customers that are willing to pay*

*Who are their competitors?*

- *In the social media market, major competitors include Facebook, Twitter, and Snapchat*

- *In the job search and recruiting market, major competitors include Indeed, Glassdoor, CareerBuilder, and ZipRecruiter*

- *In the advertising market, major competitors include Google, Facebook, and Microsoft*

- *In the online learning market, major competitors include Coursera, Khan Academy, Udemy, and Skillshare*

*What are the significant events that have happened at the company over the past few years?*

- *2016: Microsoft acquires LinkedIn, but allows LinkedIn to retain its distinct brand, culture, and independence*

- *2018: LinkedIn acquires Glint, a company that uses machine learning to analyze employees to improve employee engagement*

- *2019: LinkedIn launches the Open for Business feature to enable small businesses and freelancers to be discovered on the platform for services they offer*

- *2019: LinkedIn launches LinkedIn Events, which provides members an easy way to create and join professional events*

- *2019: LinkedIn acquires Drawbridge, a company that uses machine learning to understand customers better, to integrate with LinkedIn's marketing services to target audiences better*

*Strengths*

- *Competitive advantage lies in its massive user base of over 600 million users, which is difficult to replicate*

- *Strong network effects since the value of LinkedIn to users increases as the number of users increases*

- *Diversified revenue streams coming from three different products*

- *Strong content business with articles and posts written by professional leaders and influencers around the world*

- *A tremendous amount of data on employees and companies to identify unmet needs*

*Weaknesses*

- *LinkedIn's users have much less engagement on the platform than other social networks*

- *Only 20% of users are paying customers*

- *LinkedIn's mix of premium offerings is confusing and unclear to many potential customers*

- *Allegations of the company's invasion of privacy have hurt LinkedIn's brand name*

*Opportunities*

- *Opportunity to further increase user base by targeting more blue-collar workers*

- *Opportunity to increase the percentage of paying users by improving the Premium subscription offering*

- *Opportunity to replace headhunting and recruiting companies if LinkedIn decides to enter the recruiting-as-a-service business*

- *Opportunity to increase user engagement on the platform to increase the value of its advertising business*

*Threats*

- *Other large social media platforms (e.g., Facebook) may eventually enter the job search and recruiting markets*

- *Smaller, niche professional networks (e.g., minority networks) may better meet a customer segment's needs*

- *Difficulty balancing the different needs of job seekers and recruiters when creating and selling premium offerings*

- *Challenges in managing more fraudulent and uncredible accounts as the user base grows*

*What are the responsibilities or tasks of the role?*

- *Work with cross-functional teams to build and launch products globally, from initial market validation, positioning and messaging, to go-to-market strategy and launch execution*

- *Own user and product insights to build data-driven, actionable insights that inform product strategy*

- *Partner with digital marketing teams to test new channels to increase customer engagement or drive customer acquisition*

- *Develop sales enablement strategies*

*What skills or attributes are preferred or required?*

- *Execute and scale high impact, multi-channel go-to-market efforts for business-to-business solutions*

- *Work autonomously, focusing on critical outcomes amidst competing priorities and tight deadlines*

- *Inspire and lead cross-functional teams*

- *Use market research to inform product development strategies*

*How does the role fit with the broader organization?*

- *Work with product managers, data scientists, engineers, marketers, and salespeople to build and launch products*

- *Product marketing managers are organized into product-specific and segment-specific teams*

*What are the primary goals or targets of the team?*

- *Drive acquisition of new customers and deeper engagement among existing customers*

*What is the culture of the team and company like?*

- *Culture of people who want to change the world*

- *A transparent company with bi-weekly all-hands meetings in which the CEO gives updates and answers questions*

- *LinkedIn provides InDays each month to allow employees to focus on themselves, the company, and the world*

- *Speaker Series exposes employees to inspiring ideas and innovative thinkers from around the globe*

# Summary

- There are four different sources of information you should consider looking at when conducting research:

    o   10-K annual reports

    o   Tech articles

    o   Current and former employees

    o   Analyst reports

- There are seven essential objective pieces of information you need to know:

    o   What markets does the company play in?

    o   What is their mission statement or aspiration?

    o   What are their products and services and what percentage of total revenue do they make up?

    o   Who are their customers?

    o   What is their business model?

    o   Who are their competitors?

    o   What are the significant events that have happened at the company over the past few years?

- Use a SWOT analysis to build a perspective on the company

    o   **Strengths**: What do they do well? What qualities separate them from competitors?

    o   **Weaknesses**: What do they do poorly? What are the things that competitors do better?

- o **Opportunities**: Where are the opportunities for growth or improvement?

- o **Threats**: Who are the most threatening competitors? What are the major risks to the company's business?

- There are five essential questions you should know regarding the role and team you are interviewing for:

  - o What are the responsibilities or tasks of the role?

  - o What skills or attributes are preferred or required?

  - o How does the role fit with the broader organization?

  - o What are the primary goals or targets of the team?

  - o What is the culture of the team and company like?

## Practice

1. For the company you are interviewing for, complete the company research process.

# Behavioral & Resume Questions

## What are behavioral questions?

Behavioral questions are the most commonly asked questions. Expect to get asked at least a couple of these.

Behavioral questions ask you to draw upon a time or experience in the past in which you demonstrated a particular skill or trait. Examples of behavioral questions include the following:

- Tell me about a time when you used data to solve a problem

- Give a time when you disagreed with your manager

- What accomplishment are you most proud of?

- Describe a situation in which you handled conflict while working on a team

- What is a piece of feedback you have received from a former supervisor or colleague?

These types of questions are a way for interviewers to dive deeper beyond what is listed on your resume. It allows interviewers to understand you better on a deeper, more personal level.

# What are interviewers looking for?

Behavioral questions assess three different things.

First, behavioral questions use past behavior to determine future performance or success. Since the candidate draws upon previous experiences and actions they have taken, interviewers can get a sense of how the candidate would perform on the job.

Second, behavioral questions assess how well candidates can communicate. Does the candidate explain their experiences clearly and articulately? Does the candidate keep their stories concise?

Third, these questions can reveal a candidate's personality and cultural fit with the firm. In answering behavioral questions, candidates show characteristics, such as being confident, humble, friendly, or collaborative. Candidates can also reveal the values and morals that they believe in.

Taking these three things into account, focus on demonstrating the following three qualities:

- Show evidence of impressive, tangible accomplishments

- Communicate clearly, concisely, and confidently

- Demonstrate personality and cultural fit with the firm

You can work on the first quality by quantifying your accomplishments and explaining the impact of your work.

Don't just explain what you did and how you did it. Explain the impact and effect you had on the organization. What was the magnitude of the impact? How many people were affected? How did this impact annual revenues or costs?

*Example: Don't just say that you worked with others to analyze survey responses to identify customer improvement areas. Instead, say that you led an eight-person analytics team to analyze over 100K survey responses to identify improvement initiatives worth $200M in annual revenue.*

You can work on the second quality through practice. The more behavioral questions you practice answering, the better you will get at telling stories about your past experiences. You will stumble less often when speaking and sound more confident.

You can work on the third quality by focusing on drawing upon experiences that best fit with the culture of the firm. From conducting company research, you should have a sense of what traits the company you are interviewing for values.

*Example: If the company values collaboration, focus on drawing upon experiences in which you worked on a team or with multiple teams. If the company values innovation, focus on drawing upon experiences in which you changed the status quo.*

## What is the best way to answer behavioral questions?

There are hundreds of different behavioral questions you could get asked. Preparing specific answers for each potential behavioral question is not practical or feasible. Instead, I recommend an alternative approach that is much more efficient and effective.

Prepare 6 – 8 different stories drawn upon your past professional and personal experiences. Select experiences that are the most impressive, impactful, or unique.

Additionally, ensure that your stories are collectively diverse. For example, you don't want to have eight stories all about leadership. Instead, have at least one story for each of the following themes:

- Leadership

- Teamwork

- Problem Solving

- Resilience

- Integrity

- Decision Making

- Communication

- Interpersonal Skills

You may have some stories that can fit under several themes.

When asked a behavioral question, mentally run through your list of prepared stories and select the story that is the most relevant.

You may need to adapt, reframe, or tailor your story to ensure that it emphasizes and focuses on the theme that the specific behavioral question is asking for.

When you get asked another behavioral question, mentally run through your prepared list of stories and select the story that is the most relevant that you have not shared yet.

This strategy for behavioral questions has three main advantages.

One, it is an efficient strategy to use because you only need to prepare 6 – 8 stories instead of hundreds of stories for the hundreds of potential behavioral questions.

Two, this strategy ensures that your mind will not go blank during an interview. You will be doing very minimal thinking on the spot because you will always have a prepared list of stories to share.

Three, this strategy ensures that you are sharing only the most impressive, impactful, or unique experiences. These stories are the ones that best highlight your traits and accomplishments.

Next, we'll discuss the best way to structure your stories.

Structuring your answers to behavioral questions is crucial because it keeps your stories concise and helps you focus on the key messages that you want to deliver.

The simple but effective structure I recommend candidates use is the STAR method, which stands for Situation, Task, Action, and Result. When telling a story, go through each of these points.

**Situation**: Provide a brief overview of the situation and any context that is needed to understand the story better. Keep this section as concise as possible to make more room for the Action and Result sections, which is where you want to spend most of your time.

You may want to answer the following questions:

- When was this?

- Where were you?

- Who was involved?

*Example*: *Last year, I was working at Airbnb in their strategic planning & analysis group. I worked primarily with the customer experience team, who was responsible for overseeing customer support.*

**Task**: Describe what you were asked or required to deliver or achieve. Again, try to keep this section concise to spend more time on the Action and Results section.

You may want to answer the following questions:

- What were you asked to do?

- What was the goal or objective?

- Why was this task important?

*Example*: *I was tasked to determine whether the incremental $10M that Airbnb spent on initiatives to improve customer satisfaction had a positive return on investment. This was important because Airbnb was focused on cutting unnecessary costs to achieve better profitability.*

**Action**: Explain what steps you took to handle the task or to meet the goal or objective. Make sure that the actions center around what you specifically did. Do not focus too much on speaking to what your team did because it takes away from your accomplishment.

You may want to answer the following questions:

- What steps did you take?

- How did you take these steps?

- Why did you take these actions?

*Example: I used SQL and excel to analyze over 700K customer data points to create a model forecasting how much happy customers spend per year versus unhappy customers.*

*I collaborated with data science, customer experience, and finance teams and persuaded them to give me their support and buy-in. I also performed competitor and industry benchmarking to validate the results further.*

**Result**: Describe the outcome that your actions had, quantifying the impact and effect you had on the organization. Additionally, you can describe your key takeaways from this experience and how it impacted or influenced you as a person.

You may want to answer the following questions:

- Did you meet the goals or objectives?

- What was the outcome and impact of your actions?

- What did you learn from this experience?

- How did this experience help you grow and develop?

*Example: In the end, I determined that the customer satisfaction initiatives had a negative 20% return on investment. I presented the findings to the CFO and to my 30-person strategic planning & analysis group, who all supported my recommendation. My work would save Airbnb $10M per year moving forward.*

*Throughout this process, I learned how to work with multiple cross-functional teams and how to persuade stakeholders to get their buy-in. This experience also further reinforced my perspective on using data to make intelligent business decisions.*

# What are the questions I could get asked?

Now that you know an efficient strategy to answer any behavioral question, you should become familiar with all of the different types of behavioral questions you could get asked.

I've included a list of over forty behavioral questions below. This is not meant to be a comprehensive list of all behavioral questions, but the list will provide you with a clear idea of the different categories of behavioral questions.

Leadership questions

- Give me an example of a time when you had to lead a team

- Describe a situation in which you had to motivate someone

- Tell me about a time when you showed initiative

- Give me an example of a time when you went above and beyond the call of duty

- Tell me about a time when you had to be adaptable

Teamwork questions

- Describe a time when you had to make an individual sacrifice for the good of the team

- Tell me about a time when you worked on a highly effective team. What made the team so successful?

- What is the typical role that you take on a team?

- Can you tell me about your most recent experience working with a team?

- Give me a time when a team member wasn't doing their work. What did you do?

Problem solving questions

- Tell me about a time when you used data to solve a problem

- Describe a difficult or complicated problem that you faced. How did you approach the problem?

- Tell me about a time when you had to make a decision but did not have all of the information you needed

- Describe a time when you had too many things to do. How did you handle this?

- Give an example of a problem you solved in a unique way

Resilience questions

- Describe a situation in which you handled conflict while working on a team

- Give an example of a time when you tried to accomplish something but failed

- Describe a situation in which you made a mistake. What did you do about it?

- Tell me about a time you failed to meet a deadline. What things did you do to fail? What did you learn?

- Talk about a setback you had at work. What did you do?

Integrity questions

- Talk about a time when it was challenging to be honest

- Tell me about a time when you found out a colleague was doing something wrong. What did you do?

- Can you give me a situation in which you thought it was better to be dishonest?

- Describe a time when you followed a rule that you didn't agree with

- Can you describe a time when a colleague questioned your honesty? What did you do?

Decision making questions

- Walk me through the steps you took to make an important decision you made at work

- Tell me about a time when you had to make an immediate decision without having all the information you need

- Give me an example of a time when you made a decision that wasn't popular

- Describe a decision that you regretted making. Why did you regret it?

- Give me a time when you had to make a difficult decision

Communication questions

- Describe a time when you had to give a presentation without any preparation

- Talk about a time when your communication failed. What was the problem? How did you handle it?

- How did you communicate with your previous bosses?

- Give me an example of a time when you gave a speech or presentation for your job

- Tell me about a time when you communicated with an unresponsive person

Interpersonal skills questions

- Give a time when you disagreed with your manager

- Describe a time you disagreed with a teammate

- Tell me about a time when you had to persuade someone on a particular course of action

- How have you maintained relationships with your former managers and coworkers?

- Was there ever a time you didn't get along with a colleague? What did you do?

Other questions

- What is your greatest strength?

- What is a piece of feedback you have received from a former supervisor or colleague?

- What do you see as your weaknesses?

- What is an accomplishment that you are proud of that is not on your resume?

- What is something we should know about you that is not on your resume?

# Examples of answers to behavioral questions

**Example #1**: Describe a time when you went above and beyond the call of duty.

*While working at Apple in their AppleCare business, I was responsible for analyzing data to identify opportunities to improve customer satisfaction.*

*While looking through survey responses, I realized there was an opportunity to use the tremendous amount of data that Apple had to predict which customers were likely to cancel their AppleCare subscriptions.*

*Apple could focus on retaining these customers by sending them discount codes for renewal. I raised this point to my director and proposed taking on this project.*

*Outside of my regular job responsibilities, I pulled over five years of purchasing data for over 10 million customers to create a logistic regression model. I verified my model with data scientists and got the buy-in of members of the AppleCare strategy team.*

*In the end, I determined that Apple could increase revenues by $100M by targeting the top 10% of customers that were most likely to cancel and sending them discount codes.*

*I presented my results to the head of AppleCare, who approved testing this promotional campaign to a few cities. My director was appreciative of me going above and beyond what was required in my role.*

**Example #2**: Can you talk about a time when it was challenging to be honest?

*On my last project, I worked with a newly hired manager that was difficult to work with. He had an investment banking background and liked to overwork his team without taking breaks. We often would be expected to skip lunch to deliver work on-time.*

*The three other members of the team and I were miserable for the first two weeks working with him. After two weeks, the manager asked his direct reports for feedback on how things were going.*

*The three other members of the team were fearful of providing harsh feedback to the manager. Promotions were coming up in a few months and an unhappy manager could potentially write poor performance reviews for the team.*

*During my feedback session with the manager, I found it difficult to be honest in saying how things were going. However, I took a risk and decided to be honest. I explained that I felt that his working style was not a good fit for the team.*

*I explained that it was unhealthy to skip meals and that this made the team hungry, unhappy, and unproductive. I asked if we could be more thoughtful in prioritizing work and reducing the amount of time spent working on tasks that were not critically important. I also proposed scheduling breaks for the team to relax together, which could improve productivity later.*

*The manager was surprisingly receptive to the feedback. He explained that this was his first corporate role and that he was still adjusting to the company culture and expectations.*

*As a result, the manager took my suggestions. The team immediately became happier and more motivated. We completed the project on-time without working on any weekends by focusing on the most important tasks.*

**Example #3**: Describe a time when you had to motivate someone.

*While working on a customer service improvement project for Amazon, I led a four-person analytics team. The goal was to analyze recent customer survey data to identify ways to improve customer service.*

*I distributed work according to each person's interests and expertise. After a few weeks, I observed that three members worked productively and effectively while one member, John, was consistently delivering work that was both low-quality and late.*

*Realizing that this was a potential motivation issue, I sat down with John to understand what the root cause was. The problem was that the analytics team had recently shifted to using an analytics software called Tableau.*

*John found Tableau difficult to set up and use, so he was unmotivated to switch from using Excel, which he was an expert at. As a result, Excel could not handle the millions of rows of data, causing poor work quality and delays.*

*To motivate John, I set up three one-on-one Tableau training sessions with him to walk him through the setup of Tableau. I demonstrated how it could save him time because it performed computationally intensive calculations much quicker than Excel.*

*Afterward, John began liking Tableau. He became excited to learn about what other features of Tableau could save him time in his other projects. His performance significantly improved and he began consistently delivering high-quality work on-time.*

## The "walk me through your resume" question

Besides behavioral questions, the other most common question you'll be asked in an interview is the "walk me through your resume" question.

This question is most commonly asked at the beginning of the interview, so you should prepare for it to make a great first impression with the interviewer.

In asking this question, interviewers are looking to learn two things.

One, they want to get a quick overview of your work experience and achievements. Often, interviewers don't have the time to look through your resume before the interview.

Two, they want to understand why you are suited for the role and why you are interested in working at the company. The "walk me through your resume" question is a quick way to assess this.

Therefore, in answering this question, follow this strategy:

1. Start with a strong opening statement that summarizes your areas of expertise and number of years of experience

2. Highlight your most relevant and impressive experiences and accomplishments, starting with the most recent

3. Connect your experiences to why you're interested in the role and why you would be a good fit

Let's take a look at a few examples of how candidates walk interviewers through their resume.

**Example #1**: Walk me through your resume.

*I am a marketing and strategy professional with over seven years of experience in media and e-commerce.*

*I spent the last five years working at Activision Blizzard, where I led social media marketing. I planned and executed marketing campaigns that led to over $1 million in sales. I also developed a marketing strategy that lowered customer acquisition costs by 15%.*

*Before that, I spent two years working at LinkedIn in their ads team. I ran customer surveys and focus groups to identify key customer pain points for ad purchasers. From this, I launched over fifty tailored email campaigns that had a 25% higher conversion rate than previous campaigns.*

*Given my experience in data-driven marketing and strategy, I believe I would be an excellent fit for a product marketing manager role at Amazon.*

**Example #2**: Walk me through your resume.

*I am currently a management consultant at the Boston Consulting Group and have three years of experience working on a variety of strategic and operational projects.*

*On the strategy side, I advised a telecom client on potential adjacent markets to enter. This translated to an expected revenue growth of 20% per year over the next five years.*

*On the operations side, I helped an airline company identify over $200M in annual cost savings by adjusting their flight schedules and passenger*

*capacity. I also worked with a utility company on a pricing strategy to increase incremental revenues by 15% per year.*

*These experiences have helped me build a strategic and operational toolkit. I believe this toolkit would make me an exceptional fit for tackling the challenging business problems at Adobe. I am passionate about using my skills to drive immediate, tangible impacts for Adobe and its customers.*

**Example #3**: Walk me through your resume.

*I am a senior at Duke University, majoring in electrical and computer engineering with a passion for technology.*

*Last summer, I worked at IBM as a business development intern. I collaborated with over ten sales members to generate over $700K in potential sales leads.*

*Before that, I worked in a biology research lab that focuses on using machine learning to identify potential tumors from ultrasound images. I worked on a project to improve tumor identification algorithm accuracy by over 50% for select use cases.*

*I want to continue building on my work experiences and believe Google would be a great fit for me. I am excited about potentially working as a business analyst so that I can take on increased responsibilities and make a meaningful impact.*

# Summary

Behavioral questions

- Focus on demonstrating the following three qualities when answering behavioral questions:

    o Show evidence of impressive, tangible accomplishments

    o Communicate clearly, concisely, and confidently

    o Demonstrate your personality and cultural fit with the firm

- Prepare 6 – 8 different stories drawn upon your past professional and personal experiences

- Ensure that your stories are collectively diverse and cover a variety of different themes, such as:

    o Leadership

    o Teamwork

    o Problem solving

    o Resilience

    o Integrity

    o Decision making

    o Communication

    o Interpersonal skills

- When asked a behavioral question, mentally run through your prepared list of stories and select the one that is the most relevant that you have not shared yet

- Structure your answer using the STAR method

  - **Situation**: Provide an overview of the situation and any context needed to understand the story better

  - **Task**: Describe what you were asked to deliver

  - **Action**: Explain the different steps you took to meet the goal or objective

  - **Result**: Describe the outcome and impact of your actions and how it influenced you as a person

"Walk me through your resume" question

- Start with a strong opening statement that summarizes your areas of expertise and number of years of experience

- Highlight your most relevant and impressive experiences and accomplishments, starting with the most recent

- Connect your experiences to why you're interested in and well-suited for the role

# Practice

1. Walk me through your resume.

2. Tell me about a time when you used data to solve a problem.

3. Describe a situation in which you handled conflict while working on a team.

4. Give an example of a time when you tried to accomplish something, but failed.

5. Tell me about a time when you had to make a difficult decision.

6. What is a piece of feedback you have received from a former supervisor or colleague?

# Motivational Questions

## What are motivational questions?

You are almost certainly going to be asked at least one motivational question at some point during your interview. These questions are just as common as behavioral questions.

There are three different motivational questions that you should prepare for. In order of frequency, they are:

1. Why do you want to work at this company?

2. Why are you interested in this role?

3. Why are you interested in tech?

## What are interviewers looking for?

Interviewers primarily ask motivational questions for three reasons.

One, interviewers want to assess how interested and passionate you are about the job. Conducting interviews is time-consuming for interviewers, so they want to quickly filter out people that are not interested in the job.

By asking motivational questions, interviewers can quickly narrow the candidate pool to those that would be likely to accept the job offer. Interviewers can also get a sense of who is likely to stay in the role for a longer time.

Two, by asking for your interests, interviewers can assess whether your interests align with the missions, values, and responsibilities of the job. If what you are looking for does not align with the company or role, then you are likely a poor fit.

Three, motivational questions assess how well candidates can communicate. Does the candidate explain their interests and motivations clearly and articulately? Does the candidate keep their answers concise?

Even if you are genuinely passionate about the job and are a good fit for the role, poor communication will make it difficult for the interviewer to see this.

Taking these things into account, focus on demonstrating the following three qualities:

- Express genuine and credible interest and passion

- Demonstrate cultural fit with the firm

- Communicate clearly, concisely, and confidently

Let's walk through each of the different motivational questions to understand how to answer each best.

## Why do you want to work at this company?

There are a variety of reasons you could provide for why you are interested in working at a particular company. Select three compelling reasons for your answer.

I recommend using the following simple but effective structure when answering this question:

*"[Company Name] is a top choice for me for three reasons. One… Two… Three… For these reasons, I would love to work for [Company Name]."*

If the company is truly your number one choice, make sure to state that in the first sentence. This goes a long way in demonstrating your interest in the job. If the company is not your number one choice, just say that the company is a top choice for you.

Additionally, if the company has a strong mission or core value that employees strongly believe in, you should mention the mission or values of the company in your answer. Otherwise, select the three reasons that are the most compelling and credible.

Reasons you could give for why you are interested in working at a particular company include the following:

- The company has deep expertise in a particular area or is at the forefront of innovation in an area you are interested in

- The company is a leader in the industry and you want to learn from the best

- You believe strongly in the company's missions and values and want to be a part of that

- You enjoy using the company's products or services

- You've loved the people that you met from the company and would like to work with them

- The company has a culture that is fun or empowering

- The company makes substantial investments in mentorship and personal development, which you value tremendously

- The company is at an exciting stage of growth or turnaround and you are excited about the opportunity to make an impact

- Several mentors that you respect and look up to have worked at the company and recommended working there

Let's look at a few examples of how candidates answer this question.

**Example #1**: Why do you want to work at LinkedIn?

*LinkedIn is my top choice company to work at. There are three reasons why I'm excited about LinkedIn.*

*One, I am passionate about LinkedIn's mission of creating economic opportunity. Throughout my career, I have found tremendous fulfillment in mentoring and coaching others in their professional development. I would love to further this passion by working at a company that focuses on connecting professionals and making them more productive and successful.*

*Two, I appreciate LinkedIn's strong company culture. Everyone that I have talked to at LinkedIn emphasizes how all of the employees are friendly, supportive, and hardworking. There is an expectation of taking ownership and making a real difference. I feel that I would thrive in this type of working culture.*

*Three, LinkedIn makes serious investments in employee development through various training programs and mentorship. I value professional development tremendously because I always want to learn new things and get better at what I do.*

*For these reasons, I would love to work at LinkedIn.*

**Example #2**: Why do you want to work at Netflix?

*Netflix is a top choice for me for three reasons.*

*One, I am excited about the potential career advancement at Netflix. Unlike other tech companies, Netflix has a very transparent and structured promotion process and operates like a meritocracy. I value the potential promotion opportunities.*

*Two, the people that I've met that work at Netflix are among the smartest people I know. Everyone that I have met has had a very impressive background and list of achievements. I am excited to be potentially working with these people because I know I will learn a lot from them.*

*Three, I love using Netflix. It is something I use every day that brings great entertainment and joy in my life. I'd love to work for a company in which I use their product every day.*

*For these reasons, I am excited to have the opportunity to interview for such a great company.*

**Example #3**: Why do you want to work at Instacart?

*There are three primary reasons why I'm excited about Instacart.*

*One, I believe that Instacart is going through an exciting time of rapid growth, with new cities being added daily. I want to be a part of this process to learn how companies can grow so quickly and successfully.*

*Two, I am excited about the potential impact I can make at Instacart, which has the potential to touch over 80% of U.S. households. I want to improve the grocery shopping process for families, saving them time and money.*

*Three, I have enjoyed everyone that I have met from Instacart. They have been incredibly supportive in taking the time to answer my questions and in encouraging me to apply. I would love to work alongside these people.*

*For these reasons, I am very interested in working at Instacart.*

# Why are you interested in this role?

Again, there are many different reasons you could provide for why you are interested in the role. Select three compelling reasons for your answer.

Your reasons should focus on the responsibilities and potential impact of the role.

In other words, what parts of the job description make you excited? What responsibilities of the role make you feel fulfilled? What kind of impact are you looking to make?

Use the following simple but effective structure when answering this question:

*"I am interested in this particular role for three reasons. One... Two... Three... Given these interests, I believe I would be a great fit for the role."*

Reasons you could give for why you are interested in the role include the following:

- You value the high level of autonomy and responsibility that the role affords you

- You are excited about the potential impact you can make in the role

- The challenging problems that you would face in this role fascinate your intellectual curiosity

- You like collaborating with cross-functional teams

- You enjoy managing a team and developing team members

- You find excitement in analyzing data to find insights to make tough decisions

- You find fulfillment in providing strategic, high-level guidance and recommendations

- You take pride in solving tangible problems in which you can directly see the impact of your work

Let's look at a few examples of how candidates answer this question.

**Example #1**: Why are you interested in product management?

*I'm interested in product management for three reasons.*

*One, I find fulfillment in having tremendous responsibility and ownership over a product or part of a product. This responsibility motivates me to work hard and makes me excited about work.*

*Two, I enjoy the cross-functional nature of the role. I like collaborating with different teams and get energy from working with a diverse group of people.*

*Three, I am excited to see the real and tangible impact that I make from my work. I get fulfillment from not only setting the strategy but seeing the strategy through to execution and implementation.*

*Given these interests, I believe I would be a fantastic fit for this product management role.*

**Example #2**: Why are you interested in a strategy and business operations role?

*There are three reasons why I'm interested in this strategy and business operations role.*

*One, I enjoy the strategic, high-level thinking required to set a direction or roadmap for the company.*

*Two, I get energy from working with different business units in a company. I enjoy the camaraderie of collaborating with others in the pursuit of a common goal.*

*Three, I look forward to the potential impact I can make in this role. I am excited that my work and recommendations could affect the entire company's performance and trajectory.*

*Because of this, I am very passionate about taking a role in strategy and business operations.*

**Example #3**: Why are you interested in an analytics role?

*There are three major aspects of an analytics role that I am excited about.*

*One, I enjoy working with a tremendous amount of data. I like analyzing data to find the critical insights needed to make tough business decisions.*

*Two, I like the autonomy that comes with an analytics role. I find it empowering to have full ownership and control in the types of analyses that I do and the way that I do them.*

*Three, I am excited to see the impact of my data-driven recommendations. I find fulfillment in making a tangible difference.*

*These are the reasons why I believe an analytics role is a perfect fit for me.*

## Why are you interested in tech?

While the previous two motivational questions have a lot of flexibility in how you answer them, your answer to this question should focus on the aspirational nature of tech.

In other words, speak to how technology impacts billions of people around the world. Talk about how technology solves challenging problems and improves the quality of life. Discuss how technology influences our behaviors in the products we use every day.

You can speak to the aspirational nature of tech in the following different ways:

- You enjoy working in a fast-paced industry that is continuously changing and evolving

- You are excited to work on products that people enjoy using every day

- You are excited to work on products that can save and transform lives

- You are fascinated about the potential use cases of technology in society

- You want to play a role in moving the world forward

- You enjoy the variety of exciting challenges in tech

Afterward, connect this interest in tech to the company. How does working at this particular company fulfill your interest in tech?

Let's look at a few examples of how candidates answer this question.

**Example #1**: Why are you interested in tech? (Google)

*I am interested in tech because of its potential to improve the quality of life for billions of people around the world. There is nearly limitless potential for tech to make life easier, more efficient, and more fulfilling. I am fascinated by all of the different ways that tech can benefit society. At Google, I can contribute my part in helping move society forward.*

**Example #2**: Why are you interested in tech? (Apple)

*I am interested in tech because I am excited to work on products that people enjoy using every day. I want to see the impact of the work that I do in everyday life and how it affects people. At Apple, I have the incredible opportunity to work on products that people love to use.*

**Example #3**: Why are you interested in tech? (Facebook)

*I am interested in tech because tech is fast-paced and is constantly innovating and changing. I want to be at the forefront of this and tackle the most difficult problems. These tough problems in tech are what gives me excitement and fulfillment in my work. At Facebook, I will have the opportunity to tackle challenging but rewarding problems.*

# Summary

Motivational questions

- The three motivational questions that you should prepare for are the following:

    o Why do you want to work at this company?

    o Why are you interested in this role?

    o Why are you interested in tech?

- Focus on demonstrating the following three qualities when answering these questions

    o Express genuine and credible interest and passion

    o Demonstrate cultural fit with the firm

    o Communicate clearly, concisely, and confidently

Why do you want to work at this company?

- Use the structure: *"[Company Name] is a top choice for me for three reasons. One... Two... Three... For these reasons, I would love to work for [Company Name]"*

- If the company is truly your number one choice, make sure to state it in your first sentence

- If the company has a strong mission or core value, ensure you mention it in your answer

Why are you interested in this role?

- Use the structure: *"I am interested in this particular role for three reasons. One... Two... Three... Given these interests, I believe I would be a great fit for the role"*

- Your reasons should focus on the responsibilities and the potential impact of the role

Why are you interested in tech?

- Speak to the aspirational nature of tech

- Connect your interest in tech to your interest in the company

## Practice

For the company you are interviewing with:

1. Why do you want to work at this company?

2. Why are you interested in this role?

3. Why are you interested in tech?

# Case Interviews

# Case Interview Strategy

## What is a case interview?

Case interviews are a special type of interview question that is typically used by management consulting companies, such as McKinsey, BCG, and Bain, to assess candidates.

There are many people in tech that come from a management consulting background. Therefore, some of your interviews, especially those for strategy and business operations roles, may include a case interview.

A case interview, or "case," is a 30- to 45-minute exercise in which you and the interviewer work together to develop a recommendation to answer or solve a business problem.

These business problems can be anything that real companies face. A few examples are:

- What should Netflix do to increase customer retention?

- How should Apple price its new iPhone?

- How can Intel improve its profit margins?

- Should Facebook acquire another artificial intelligence startup?

- Which country should Amazon expand to next?

At the beginning of the interview, the interviewer will give you background information and the business problem. In the end, you'll present a recommendation and provide 2 – 3 reasons that support your recommendation.

These 2 – 3 reasons will likely be both quantitative and qualitative. You may need to interpret charts and graphs, perform calculations, brainstorm ideas, and have qualitative discussions.

There usually is no single right answer for a case. As long as you have logical reasons and evidence that support your recommendations, you will do well.

Although there are many business problems you could be asked to solve, almost all case interviews follow the same format or structure. Therefore, you can use the same strategies for every case interview.

## What are interviewers looking for?

In just a 30- to 45- minute case interview, interviewers can assess many different skills and competencies. There are five main qualities that interviewers are looking for.

1. **Logical, structured thinking**: Can you structure complex problems in a clear and simple way? Can you identify the most critical points from large quantities of information? Can you use logic and reason to make appropriate conclusions?

2. **Analytical problem solving**: Can you perform math calculations quickly and easily? Can you analyze data effectively to drive insights? Can you set up and solve equations to determine financial implications?

3. **Business acumen**: Do your recommendations make sense from a business perspective? Do you have a solid understanding of business concepts and principles?

4. **Communication skills**: Can you communicate in a clear, concise way? Are you easy to understand and follow?

5. **Personality and cultural fit**: Are you collaborative, coachable, easy to work with, and friendly?

Later in this chapter, we'll go through each step of a case interview and learn the most effective strategies to demonstrate these qualities.

# Example of a case interview

There are seven main parts of a case interview:

- Understanding the case background information

- Asking clarifying questions

- Structuring a framework

- Starting the case

- Solving quantitative problems

- Answering qualitative questions

- Delivering a recommendation

To best illustrate exactly how a case interview might look like, let's go through a full case interview to see each of these parts in action.

*Interviewer: Facebook is an online social media and social networking service with about $70 billion in annual revenue, $20 billion in annual profit, and 2.5 billion users. They are looking to grow and are considering entering the global smartphone market. Should they enter?*

*Candidate*: To make sure I understand correctly, Facebook is looking to grow and is considering entering the global smartphone market. Our objective is to determine whether or not they should enter.

*Interviewer*: Correct.

*Candidate*: Is Facebook looking to grow revenues or profits?

*Interviewer*: Facebook wants to grow profits.

*Candidate*: Is there a particular financial goal or metric that Facebook is trying to reach within a specific time frame?

*Interviewer*: They are looking to grow annual profits by $10 billion over the next five years.

*Candidate*: Great. Those are all the questions I have for now. Would you mind if I take a few minutes to structure my thoughts and develop a framework to tackle this case?

*Interviewer*: Sure, go ahead.

*(2 - 3 minutes of silence pass)*

*Candidate*: To decide whether or not Facebook should enter the global smartphone market, I want to look into four main areas.

One, I want to look into the smartphone market attractiveness. Is this an attractive market to enter? I want to look into areas such as market size, growth rate, and profit margins.

Two, I want to look into the smartphone competitive landscape. Is this market competitive, and will Facebook be able to capture a meaningful market share? I want to look into questions such as the number of competitors, how much market share each competitor has, and whether competitors have any competitive advantages.

Three, I want to look into Facebook's capabilities. Do they have the capabilities to succeed in the smartphone market? I want to look into things such as whether they have the expertise to make smartphones, whether they *have the distribution channels to sell them, and whether there are any existing synergies they can leverage.*

*Four, I want to look into expected profitability. Will Facebook be profitable from entering this market? I want to look into areas such as the expected revenues, the expected costs, and how long it would take to break even.*

***Interviewer***: *Your framework makes sense to me. Where should we start?*

***Candidate***: *Perhaps we can start by looking at the smartphone market attractiveness.*

***Interviewer***: *Okay. Let's start by estimating the global market size of smartphones.*

***Candidate***: *To estimate the global market size of smartphones, I'm going to start with the global population. Then I'll estimate the percentage that has mobile phones. Next, I'll estimate what percentage of those phones are smartphones.*

*If we take this and multiply it by the frequency in which people buy smartphones and the average price of a smartphone, we'll find an estimate for the global market size.*

*Does this approach make sense to you?*

***Interviewer***: *Makes sense to me.*

***Candidate***: *Great. I'll assume the global population is about 8 billion people. If 75% of people in the world have some kind of mobile phone, that means 6 billion people have a mobile phone.*

*Let's assume that 80% of mobile phones are smartphones. That means there are 4.8 billion smartphones.*

*The average person purchases a new smartphone about once every three years. Therefore, 1.6 billion smartphones are purchased each year.*

*If the average smartphone is priced at $500, that means the global market size of smartphones is roughly $800 billion.*

**Interviewer**: *Those seem like reasonable assumptions.*

**Candidate**: *Given that Facebook has annual revenues of $70 billion, an $800 billion smartphone market represents a massive opportunity.*

*The sheer size makes the smartphone market look attractive, but I'd like to understand if smartphone margins are typically high and determine how much market share Facebook could realistically capture.*

**Interviewer**: *Let's go with your assumption that smartphones, on average, are priced at $500. Assume smartphone margins are 20% and that annual fixed costs for production, marketing, and distribution are $32 billion.*

*How much market share would Facebook need to capture to break even?*

**Candidate**: *To determine the breakeven point, I'll compute how much profit each smartphone contributes. Then, I'll divide the total annual fixed costs by this amount to determine how many smartphones Facebook needs to sell each year.*

*I previously calculated that 1.6 billion smartphones are sold each year, so I can divide the number of phones Facebook needs to sell each year by 1.6 billion smartphones to determine how much market share they need.*

**Interviewer**: *Great. Let's proceed.*

**Candidate**: *On average, smartphones are $500, with a margin of 20%. Therefore, Facebook makes $100 in profit per phone sold. Dividing the annual fixed costs of $32 billion by $100 gives us 320 million smartphones that need to be sold each year.*

*320 million smartphones divided by 1.6 billion smartphones is 20%. Therefore, Facebook needs to capture a 20% market share to break even.*

**Interviewer**: *Take a look at this chart. What are your takeaways?*

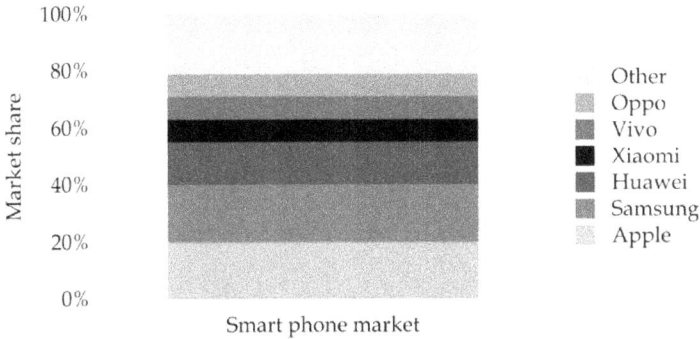

**Candidate**: *This chart shows the global market shares of smartphone players. There are two key takeaways that I see.*

*One, the smartphone market is highly concentrated. The top six players have 80% of the global market share. This implies that there are high barriers to entry and competition is likely fierce.*

*Two, the market leaders are Apple and Samsung, which each have a 20% market share. We previously calculated that Facebook would need a 20% market share to break even. This is likely difficult to achieve for a new player in the market.*

**Interviewer**: *You mentioned that barriers to entry are high. What are the major barriers to entry in the smartphone market?*

**Candidate**: *I'm thinking of barriers to entry as economic barriers and non-economic barriers. Economic barriers include things such as production equipment, electronic parts, and other capital. Non-economic barriers include expertise, brand name, and distribution channels.*

**Interviewer**: *Do you think Facebook can overcome these barriers to entry?*

**Candidate**: *I don't think Facebook can overcome these barriers for the following two reasons.*

*One, Facebook has minimal experience producing hardware products, so they likely don't have the right people and expertise to make smartphones.*

*Two, Facebook has no existing distribution channels with smartphone retailers. Even if they could produce smartphones, it could be challenging getting customers to buy them.*

***Interviewer****: Let's say that the Facebook executive team asks you for your preliminary recommendation. What would you say?*

***Candidate****: I recommend that Facebook should not enter the global smartphone market for the following three reasons.*

*One, although the market size is massive at $800B, the smartphone market is highly concentrated. The top six players have 80% of the global market share. This implies that competition is fierce.*

*Two, Facebook would need to capture a 20% market share to break even. For comparison, the smartphone market leaders, Apple and Samsung, have 20% market share each. Therefore, this target does not seem feasible.*

*Three, barriers to entry are high and Facebook will likely not be able to overcome them. Facebook has minimal experience in producing hardware and they have no distribution channels with smartphone retailers.*

*For next steps, we can look into other adjacent markets to see which are more attractive and feasible for Facebook to pursue growth in.*

## How do I best answer case interview questions?

Now that you understand what a case looks like, let's go through each step of a case interview to learn the most effective strategies.

Before beginning, you can download a case interview cheat sheet that summarizes everything you need to memorize by emailing **conquer.interviews@gmail.com** with the subject "**Get More**". An automated email will send you all supplementary information that comes with this book.

## Understanding the case background information

The case interview begins with the interviewer giving you the case background information. As the interviewer reads through the information, take notes.

Turn your paper landscape and draw a vertical line to divide your paper into two sections. The first section should be two-thirds of the page and the second section should be one-third of the page.

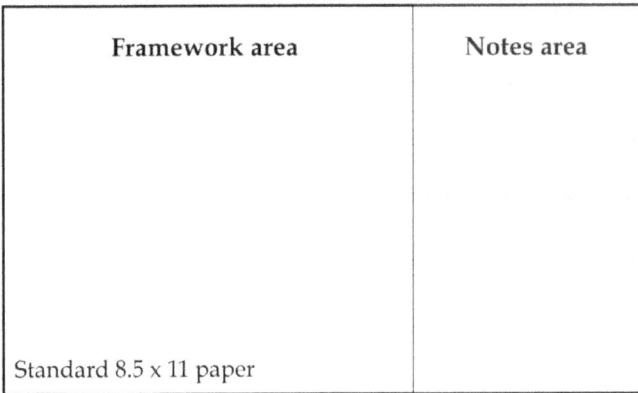

| Framework area | Notes area |
| --- | --- |
| | |
| | |
| | |
| Standard 8.5 x 11 paper | |

Take notes in the second section of the page and save the first section for your framework later.

While the interviewer is giving you the case background information, pay particularly close attention to three things:

- **Issue**: What problem or challenge is the company facing?

- **Objective**: What is the objective of the case?

- **Metric**: What is the metric that defines success?

*Example: In the previous Facebook case, Facebook faced the challenge of growing. The objective was to determine whether they should enter the smartphone market. The metric of success was increasing profits by $10 billion over five years.*

After the interviewer finishes giving the case background information, summarize the information back to the interviewer. Do not regurgitate everything verbatim. Keep your summary concise and only mention the essential pieces of information.

Additionally, verify the objective of the case. Answering or solving the wrong case objective is the quickest way to fail a case interview.

## Asking clarifying questions

After summarizing the case and confirming the objective, you'll have the opportunity to ask questions before you begin thinking about how to solve the case.

At this point, only ask questions that are critical for you to understand the case background and objective fully. You'll always be able to ask more questions later.

There are four types of questions you should focus on asking:

- Asking for a definition of an unfamiliar term

- Asking for information that strengthens your understanding of the company or situation

- Asking questions that clarify the objective of the case

- Asking to repeat information you may have missed

*Example: In the Facebook case, we asked a question to understand whether Facebook was looking to grow revenues or profits. We also asked a question to identify the success metric, which was a $10 billion profit increase over five years.*

## Structuring a framework

After asking clarifying questions, lay out a framework of what areas you want to look into to solve the case.

A framework is simply a tool that helps you structure and break down complex problems into simpler, smaller components. Think of a framework as brainstorming different ideas and organizing them into different categories.

Your framework should have 3 – 4 broad areas, which are sometimes called "buckets."

When creating a framework, it is acceptable to ask the interviewer for a few minutes of silence to write out a structure.

*Example: In the Facebook case, we used the following framework:*

- *Smartphone market attractiveness*

  - *What is the market size?*

  - *What is the market growth rate?*

  - *What are the average profit margins?*

- *Competitive landscape*

  - *How many competitors are there?*

  - *How much share do they have?*

  - *Do competitors have any competitive advantages?*

- *Facebook capabilities*

  - *Are there significant capability gaps?*

  - *Are there significant synergies that we can leverage?*

- *Profitability*

  - *What are the expected revenues and costs?*

  - *How long will it take to break even?*

So, how did we develop this framework?

Most candidates make the mistake of either using a single memorized framework for every case or memorizing multiple different frameworks for different cases.

The issue with memorized frameworks is that they aren't tailored to the specific case you are solving for. When given an atypical business problem, your framework elements will not be entirely relevant. Additionally, interviewers can tell when you are regurgitating memorized information and not thinking critically.

Instead of memorizing frameworks, I recommend memorizing a list of 8 - 10 broad business elements, such as the following:

- Market attractiveness

- Competitive landscape

- Company capabilities or company attractiveness

- Customer needs

- Profitability

- Strategic alternatives

- Risks & mitigations

- Create your own

When given a case, mentally run through this list and pick the 3 – 4 elements that are most relevant. This will be your framework.

If the list does not give you enough elements, brainstorm and add your own. This is the "create your own" element.

This strategy guarantees that your framework elements are relevant to the case. It also demonstrates that you can create unique, tailored frameworks for every business problem.

*Example*: *For the Facebook case, we selected: market attractiveness, competitive landscape, company capabilities, and profitability.*

You will write your framework in the first section of your paper.

| Framework area | Notes area |
| --- | --- |
| Standard 8.5 x 11 paper | |

When you have completed your framework, turn your paper to face the interviewer and walk them through it. The interviewer may ask a few questions on your approach, but will otherwise indicate whether they agree or disagree with your structure.

**Starting the case**

There are two styles of case interviews: interviewer-led cases and candidate-led cases.

For interviewer-led cases, the interviewer will propose which area of your framework they would like to dive deeper into.

For candidate-led cases, you will be expected to propose an area to look into. There is no right or wrong area to start in. Propose any area of your framework as long as you have a reason for it.

If you end up picking an area that the interviewer does not want you to explore, they will redirect you to focus on a different area.

*Example: In the Facebook case, we proposed starting with the market attractiveness bucket. The interviewer agreed and provided guidance to start by determining the market size.*

Interviewer-led and candidate-led cases are nearly identical. The only difference is whether or not you have to proactively propose what area to explore first and what area you want to explore next.

## Solving quantitative problems

Once the case is fully underway, you'll get a mix of quantitative problems to solve and qualitative questions to answer. In this part, we'll focus on learning how to solve quantitative problems.

There are three different types of quantitative problems:

- Market sizing questions

- Profit and breakeven questions

- Charts and graphs questions

We'll begin by looking at the most effective strategies for market sizing questions.

Most candidates jump right into the math, making assumptions and then performing various calculations. Doing math without laying out a structure often leads to making unnecessary calculations or reaching a dead-end.

Laying out an upfront approach helps avoid these mistakes and demonstrates that you are a logical, structured thinker.

*Example: In the Facebook case, we were asked to estimate the global market size of smartphones. For this problem, you could structure your approach in the following way:*

- *Start with the global population*

- *Estimate the percentage that have mobile phones*

- *Estimate the percentage that are smartphones*

- *Estimate the frequency in which people buy smartphones*

- *Estimate the average price per smartphone*

- *Multiply these steps together to get the answer*

By laying out an approach, the interviewer can easily understand how you are thinking about the problem. With the right structure, the rest of the problem is simple arithmetic.

Sometimes the interviewer will give you numbers to use for these calculations. Other times, you'll be expected to make assumptions.

Finally, make sure to do your calculations on a separate sheet of paper. Calculations often get messy and you want to keep your original paper clean and organized.

The second type of quantitative question are profit and breakeven questions. For these problems, know the basic formulas for profit.

- Profit = Revenue – Costs

- Revenue = Quantity * Price

- Costs = Total Variable Costs + Total Fixed Costs

- Total Variable Costs = Quantity * Variable Costs

Putting these equations together, we can rewrite them in the following simplified way.

Profit = (Price – Variable Costs) * Quantity – Total Fixed Costs

A breakeven point occurs when a company sells enough product such that it has exactly recouped all costs. In other words, breakeven occurs when profit is zero.

To solve for the breakeven point, simply set profit equal to zero and solve for the unknown variable in the equation. Again, make sure to structure your approach before you begin doing calculations.

*Example: For the Facebook case, we were given price, variable costs, and total fixed costs. We set profit equal to zero and solved for the remaining unknown variable, quantity.*

The third and final type of quantitative problem involves interpreting charts and graphs.

There are a variety of charts and graphs that you should be familiar with. These include:

- Bar charts

- Pie charts

- Line graphs

- Bubble charts

- Waterfall charts

- Tables

A helpful strategy in interpreting charts and graphs is to explain the axes. What does the x-axis measure? What does the y-axis measure? This will help you understand the information better.

Also, don't just read what numbers the chart or graph shows. Instead, interpret what those numbers mean for the case objective.

*Example: In the Facebook case, we did not just read off the market shares of each player. Based on the number of players in the smartphone market and their respective market shares, we drew insights on the competitiveness of the market.*

## Answering qualitative questions

In addition to asking quantitative questions, the interviewer will also ask qualitative questions. There are two types of qualitative questions, brainstorming questions and business opinion questions.

Let's look at brainstorming questions first. Most candidates answer these questions by randomly listing the ideas that immediately come to mind. This is a highly unstructured way of answering.

Instead, use a simple two-bucket framework to help facilitate brainstorming and demonstrate logic and structure. Two-bucket frameworks you can use include:

- Internal / external

- Short-term / long-term

- Economic / non-economic

- Quantitative / qualitative

- Direct / indirect

- Supply-side / demand-side

- Benefits / costs

*Example: In the Facebook case, the interviewer asked, "What are the major barriers to entry in the smartphone market?"*

*We answered this brainstorming question using an economic / non-economic framework:*

- *Economic barriers*

  o *Production equipment*

  o *Electronic parts*

- o   *Other capital*

- *Non-economic barriers*

  - o   *Smartphone expertise*

  - o   *Brand name*

  - o   *Distribution channels*

Let's look at the second type of qualitative question, business opinion questions.

For these types of questions, there is typically no single correct answer. As long as you have logical reasons and evidence that support your recommendations, you will do well.

Use the following structure to answer business opinion questions:

1.   Firmly state your opinion

2.   Provide 2 – 3 reasons to support it

This structure will help you communicate clearly and concisely.

**Example**: *In the Facebook case, the interviewer asked, "Do you think Facebook can overcome these barriers to entry?"*

*We answered that Facebook would not be able to overcome these barriers due to two reasons. One, Facebook has minimal experience producing hardware products. Two, Facebook has no existing distribution channels with smartphone retailers.*

## Delivering a recommendation

At the end of the case interview, you will be asked to deliver your final recommendation. This is an opportunity to put together all of the work you have done so far.

Throughout the interview, you should be writing down the key takeaways. Look through your key takeaways and decide what recommendation they collectively support.

*Example*: *For the Facebook case, we had the following key takeaways:*

- *The global smartphone market is massive at $800 billion*

- *Facebook needs to capture 20% market share to break even*

- *The smartphone market is concentrated with the top six players having 80% of the total market share, suggesting high barriers to entry and fierce competition*

- *The market leaders are Apple and Samsung, which each have market shares of 20%*

- *Facebook likely cannot overcome the barriers to entry, particularly smartphone expertise and distribution channels*

*Overall, these takeaways suggest that Facebook should not enter the global smartphone market.*

Use the following structure to deliver your recommendation:

1. Clearly state your recommendation

2. Provide 2 - 3 reasons that support it

3. State potential next steps

# Summary

Case interviews

- A case interview, or "case," is a 30- to 45-minute exercise in which you and the interviewer work together to develop a recommendation to answer or solve a business problem

- There are seven main parts of a case interview

  o Understanding the case background information

  o Asking clarifying questions

  o Structuring a framework

  o Starting the case

  o Solving quantitative problems

  o Answering qualitative questions

  o Delivering a recommendation

Understanding the case background information

- Take notes on the case background information, paying close attention to the issue, objective, and metric of success

- Provide a concise summary of the case background information and verify the objective

Asking clarifying questions

- There are four types of questions you should focus on asking:

  o Asking for a definition of an unfamiliar term

- Asking for information that strengthens your understanding of the company or situation

- Asking questions that clarify the objective of the case

- Asking to repeat information you may have missed

Structuring a framework

- A framework is a tool that helps you structure and break down complex problems into simpler, smaller components

- Memorize a list of 8 - 10 broad business elements:

    - Market attractiveness

    - Competitive landscape

    - Company capabilities or company attractiveness

    - Customer needs

    - Profitability

    - Strategic alternatives

    - Risks & mitigations

    - Create your own

- When given a case, mentally run through this list and pick the 3 – 4 elements that are most relevant to the case

- If the list does not give you enough elements, brainstorm and add your own elements to your framework

- Walk your interviewer through your framework

Starting the case

- There are two styles of case interviews: interviewer-led cases and candidate-led cases

- For interviewer-led cases, the interviewer will propose which area of your framework they would like to dive deeper into

- For candidate-led cases, propose any area of your framework to start with and have a reason to support your choice

Solving quantitative problems

- There are three types of quantitative problems

    o Market sizing questions

    o Profit and breakeven questions

    o Charts and graphs questions

- For market sizing questions:

    o Lay out an upfront approach to avoid making unnecessary calculations or reaching a dead-end

    o Sometimes the interviewer will give you numbers to use for calculations, but other times you'll be expected to make assumptions or estimates

- For profit and breakeven questions:

    o Profit = (Price – Variable Costs) * Quantity – Total Fixed Costs

    o Structure your approach before doing calculations

- For charts and graphs questions:

- o Start by explaining the chart axes to help you better understand the information

- o Don't just read off numbers, but interpret what they mean for the case objective

Answering qualitative questions

- There are two types of qualitative questions, brainstorming questions and business opinion questions

- Use a simple two-bucket framework when answering brainstorming questions:

  - o Internal / external

  - o Short-term / long-term

  - o Economic / non-economic

  - o Quantitative / qualitative

  - o Direct / indirect

  - o Supply-side / demand-side

  - o Benefits / costs

- Use the following structure when answering business opinion questions:

  - o Firmly state your opinion

  - o Provide 2 – 3 reasons that support it

Delivering a recommendation

- Throughout the interview, write down the key takeaways

- When asked for a recommendation, look through your key takeaways and decide what recommendation they collectively support

- Use the following structure to deliver your recommendation:

  o Clearly state your recommendation

  o Provide 2 - 3 reasons that support it

  o State potential next steps

# Case Interview Practice

## Introduction to practicing case interviews

Case interview practice is best done with a partner, who will take on the role of an interviewer. Your case partner will lead you through the case interview, provide case information to you, and question your answers and approaches.

Practicing with a partner closely simulates the actual interview because it forces you to collaborate with the interviewer to get to a recommendation. Therefore, you will get much more benefit from practicing with a partner than from practicing by yourself.

Since not everyone can find a case partner, I have written the following practice cases such that they can be done individually.

## Practice Case #1: Lyft's international expansion

Lyft is a ride-sharing application that connects passengers with drivers. In cities where Lyft operates, passengers use the app to request a ride from one destination to another.

A nearby driver will see this request and accept the passenger, driving to pick up the passenger and dropping them off at their destination. Payments are all made pre-rider pickup via credit card on the app.

Let's say that Lyft is currently only in the U.S. and is considering expanding internationally. They want to know which international city they should enter first and how they should go about entering.

## Question #1

Let's start with the first part. How would you determine which international city to enter first?

*Solution: One potential framework could look like the following:*

- *Ride-sharing market attractiveness of each city*

    o *What is smartphone adoption?*

    o *What is credit card adoption?*

    o *What is the population density?*

- *Competitive landscape in each city*

    o *Are there other ride-sharing app competitors?*

    o *How strong are alternatives to ride-sharing?*

- *Capability to execute in each city*

    o *How much familiarity does Lyft have with the city?*

    o *How similar is the city to Lyft's home markets?*

- *Expected profits in each city*

    o *How much revenue can Lyft capture?*

    o *What are the costs of launching?*

## Question #2

We've collected the following data on five different international cities. Which city is most attractive to enter?

| Statistic | Tokyo | Sydney | Paris | Mexico City | Moscow |
|---|---|---|---|---|---|
| City population | 9M | 5M | 4M | 9M | 12M |
| % roads paved | 80% | 40% | 100% | 34% | 67% |
| % credit card adoption | 58% | 62% | 64% | 13% | 10% |
| % smart phone adoption | 45% | 65% | 60% | 37% | 36% |
| Income per capita | $46K | $65K | $42K | $10K | $14K |
| Population density (people per sq mile) | 339 | 2 | 225 | 57 | 22 |
| Cellular internet speed | Fast | Average | Fast | Average | Average |

*Solution: The key is to prioritize which metrics are most important.*

- *Percentage smartphone adoption: Sydney (65%), Paris (60%), and Tokyo (45%) score the highest*

- *Percentage credit card adoption: Paris (64%), Sydney (62%), and Tokyo (58%) score the highest*

- *Population density: Tokyo (339) and Paris (225) score high*

- *Income per capita: Sydney ($65K), Tokyo ($46K), and Paris ($42K) score the highest*

*The other metrics of city population, percentage roads paved, and cellular internet speed are less important.*

*Based on this, Paris or Tokyo are the most attractive cities to enter.*

## Question #3

Assume that Lyft decides to enter Paris. How do you think about calculating the expected annual revenue?

*Solution: One potential approach to estimate the expected annual revenue could look like the following:*

- *Start with Paris city population*

- *Estimate the percentage that would use a ride-sharing app*

- *Estimate the average number of rides per week*

- *Estimate the average price per ride*

- *Convert weekly revenue to annual revenue*

- *Estimate the percent market share that Lyft will have*

## Question #4

We found that there are three distinct customer segments: urban, suburban, and rural. Which customer segment should we target?

| Segment | Population | % that use ride-sharing | Rides/ week | Price per ride | Expected market share |
|---------|-----------|-------------------------|-------------|----------------|-----------------------|
| Urban | 600K | 80% | 5 | $5 | 50% |
| Suburban | 2.2M | 50% | 2 | $7.5 | 60% |
| Rural | 1.2M | 20% | 0.5 | $40 | 75% |

*Solution: To solve this, calculate weekly revenue for each segment.*

*Urban = $600K * 80% * 5 * $5 * 50% = $6M weekly revenue*

*Suburban = 2.2M * 50% * 2 * $7.50 * 60% = $9.9M weekly revenue*

*Rural = 1.2M * 20% * 0.5 * $40 * 75% = $3.6M weekly revenue*

*Lyft should target the suburban segment since they generate the highest weekly revenue.*

## Question #5

What are the major cost elements of starting and operating a ride-sharing app business in a new city?

*Solution: We can structure our answer in the following way:*

- *Variable costs*

    o *Paying the driver for each ride*

    o *Paying for insurance for each ride*

- *Fixed costs*

    o *IT infrastructure costs for maintaining the app*

    o *Marketing costs to attract riders*

    o *Marketing costs to attract drivers*

    o *City business licenses or permits*

**Question #6**:

Let's say that we are targeting the suburban segment, which has expected annual revenues of $500 million. Variable costs are 40% of revenue. Fixed costs for five years of operation would be $600 million, which cannot be recouped.

The Paris city government could potentially begin regulating the ride-sharing market, setting regulations that Lyft must abide by.

We believe there is a 10% chance in the next five years that the government will ban all foreign ride-sharing companies. If this happens, Lyft would need to leave Paris after five years and pay a $500 million fine.

Does entering the Paris market still make sense?

*Solution: First, let's calculate the five-year profit for Lyft if they are not banned from Paris.*

*Five-year profit = (5 \* $500M \* 60%) - $600M = $900M*

*Next, we'll calculate the five-year profit for Lyft if they are banned from Paris and fined $500 million. In this scenario, Lyft would still make a five-year profit of $900 million but would need to pay a $500 million fine.*

*Five-year profit = $900M - $500M = $400M*

*Finally, we can calculate the expected value given that there is a 90% chance of being allowed to operate in Paris and a 10% chance of being banned and fined.*

*Five-year expected value = (10% \* $400M) + (90% \* $900M) = $850M*

*Entering Paris still makes sense. Lyft expects to earn $850 million in profit over five years from entering Paris based on expected value. Even in the worst-case scenario of being banned from Paris and fined, Lyft would still make $400 million in profit over five years.*

## Question #7

What is your final recommendation?

*Solution: One recommendation could look like the following:*

*I recommend that Lyft enters the Paris market, targeting the suburban segment for the following three reasons.*

*One, Paris is the most attractive city among the five cities we analyzed. Paris ranks high on key metrics, such as percentage smartphone adoption, percentage credit card adoption, and city population density.*

*Two, the suburban segment within Paris is the most attractive, with the highest expected annual revenue of $500 million.*

*Three, despite the possibility that the government could ban foreign ride-sharing companies, the expected value of entering Paris is highly positive. Lyft should expect to earn $850 million in profit over the next five years.*

*For next steps, I'd like to look into two areas. One, I'd look into the profitability of other cities to see if there is another city with more favorable government regulations and less risk. Two, I'd consider how compatible each international city is with Lyft's company capabilities.*

# Practice Case #2: Google's new market entry

Google is considering entering the video game console market.

## Question #1

What factors would you consider in deciding whether to enter?

*Solution: One potential framework could look like the following:*

- *Video game console market attractiveness*

    o *How large is the video game console market?*

- o  *What is the growth rate?*

- o  *What are the average profit margins?*

- *Video game console competitive landscape*

  - o  *How many other players sell video game consoles?*

  - o  *How much share do these players have?*

  - o  *Do these players have any competitive advantages?*

- *Google's capabilities*

  - o  *Can Google produce an outstanding console?*

  - o  *Does Google have sufficient capital?*

  - o  *Does Google have the right distribution channels?*

- *Profitability*

  - o  *Will launching a video game console be profitable?*

  - o  *How long will it take to break even?*

  - o  *Will this product cannibalize sales from other products?*

## Question #2

Your team gathered the following information on the global video game market. What share of the video game console market would Google need to capture to break even? Google believes they can capture at least 25% of the market.

| Video game market | Video game console market | Google console prices and costs |
|---|---|---|

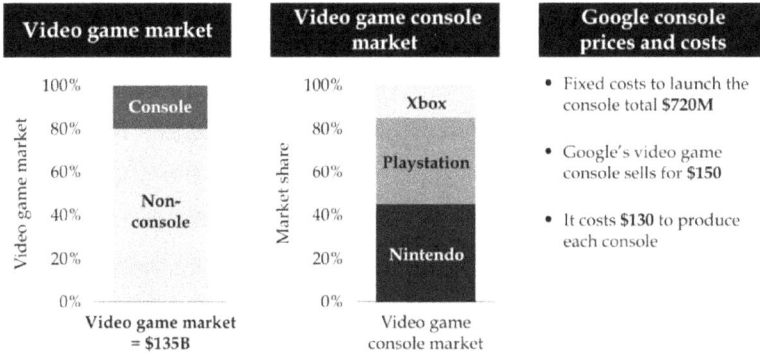

Video game market: Console, Non-console. Video game market = $135B

Video game console market: Xbox, Playstation, Nintendo. Video game console market

- Fixed costs to launch the console total **$720M**

- Google's video game console sells for **$150**

- It costs **$130** to produce each console

*Solution: To calculate the breakeven point, set the profit equation equal to zero and solve for quantity.*

*Profit = (Price – Variable Cost) * Quantity – Fixed Costs*

*$0 = ($150 - $130) * Quantity - $720M*

*Quantity = 36M units*

*Next, determine how much revenue Google needs to achieve.*

*Breakeven revenue = 36M units * $150 = $5.4B*

*Afterward, determine the video game console market size.*

*Video game console market size = $135B * 20% = $27B*

*Finally, we can calculate the market share needed to break even.*

*Breakeven market share = $5.4B / $27B = 20%*

*Google needs to capture a 20% market share to break even, requiring them to be the #3 player in the market. This is lower than the 25% market share Google expects to be able to capture.*

## Question #3

What would Google need to do to ensure it captures at least a 20% market share?

*Solution: There are three components Google should focus on to ensure it reaches its market share goals.*

- *Create a winning product*

  - *Ensure that the video game console matches the needs and preferences of customers*

  - *Ensure that the video game console is superior or differentiated from competitor products*

- *Have strong marketing and branding*

  - *Raise awareness among customers*

  - *Craft a compelling, convincing value proposition*

- *Operate efficiently*

  - *Have an effective sales force to get the product into stores*

  - *Ensure production capabilities are sufficient to produce enough units*

## Question #4

To determine how to best launch the new video game console, Google conducted a consumer survey on perceptions of competitor video game consoles and purchasing behaviors. What insights can you draw?

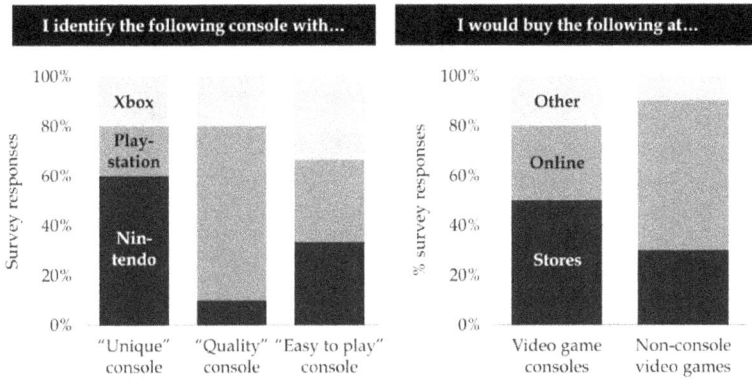

*Solution: There are two key takeaways from the charts.*

*One, Nintendo's product dominates "unique" while PlayStation's product dominates "quality." However, in the "easy to play" category, there is no clear leader. This is an opportunity for Google to differentiate its product.*

*Two, distribution channels for video game consoles are significantly different from non-console video games. Consoles are purchased more often in stores and "other." Therefore, Google needs to understand what the "other" distribution channel is and focus on that channel along with stores.*

*In summary, Google should position its product as being "easy to play" and distribute its product through stores and "other" distribution channels.*

## Question #5

What is your recommendation for Google regarding its video game console product launch?

*Solution: One recommendation could look like the following:*

*I recommend that Google enter the video game console market, focusing on creating a console that is "easy to play" while targeting stores and "other" distribution channels. Three reasons support this.*

*One, Google needs to capture 20% of the video game console market share to break even, which is less than the 25% market share it expects to achieve.*

*Two, there is an opportunity for Google to create a differentiated console to dominate the "easy to play" category because there is no clear leader there.*

*Three, Google needs to target stores and "other" distribution channels because video game console customers have significantly different purchasing behaviors than non-console video game customers.*

*For next steps, I'd like to look into two areas. One, confirm that Google will be able to achieve the 20% market share needed to break even. Two, investigate what the "other" distribution channels are and determine if Google can distribute through those channels.*

# Practice Case #3: Cisco's profitability issue

Cisco has been experiencing a decline in profitability over the past year in its IT services business.

## Question #1

How would you determine what Cisco should do to improve profitability?

*Solution: One potential framework could look like the following:*

- *Drivers of profitability*

  - *How have revenues changed?*

  - *How have costs changed?*

- *IT services competitive landscape*

  - *Have competitors done something differently?*

  - *Are there new entrants?*

    o   *Have competitors also seen a decline in profitability?*

- *Customer needs for IT services*

    o   *Have customer needs or preferences changed?*

    o   *Have customer purchasing behaviors changed?*

- *IT services market trends*

    o   *Are there new regulations affecting the market?*

    o   *Are there new disruptive technologies?*

    o   *What other trends are happening?*

## Question #2

Cisco has IT services for servers, routers, and switches. We have collected the following data on sales. What is causing the decline in profitability?

| Service | Year 1 | | | Year 2 | | |
|---|---|---|---|---|---|---|
| | % of revenue | Price | Cost | % of revenue | Price | Cost |
| Servers | 20% | $4,000 | $1,000 | 20% | $4,000 | $1,400 |
| Routers | 30% | $5,000 | $3,000 | 50% | $4,000 | $2,400 |
| Switches | 50% | $2,000 | $500 | 30% | $2,400 | $600 |

*Solution: Let's first look at profit margins for each type of service.*

*The margin for services for servers has decreased from 75% to 65%, which drives overall profitability down. The margins for services for routers and switches remain unchanged.*

*Next, let's look at the sales mix.*

*Sales of services for routers have increased from 30% to 50% of revenues while sales of services for switches have declined from 50% to 30%.*

*Since services for switches have a profit margin of 75% and services for routers have a profit margin of 40%, Cisco is selling more of a lower margin service and less of a higher margin service.*

*The decline in profitability is due to a decrease in the profit margin for services for servers and a sales mix change of selling more services for routers and fewer services for switches.*

## Question #3

How much have overall margins declined by? What is the largest driver of the decline?

*Solution: Let's calculate the profit margins for the two years.*

*Year 1 sales mix is 20% servers, 30% routers, and 50% switches. Profit margins are 75% for servers, 40% for routers, and 75% for switches.*

*Year 1 margin = (20% \* 75%) + (30% \* 40%) + (50% \* 75%) = 64.5%*

*Year 2 sales mix is 20% servers, 50% routers, and 30% switches. Profit margins are 65% for servers, 40% for routers, and 75% for switches.*

*Year 2 margin = (20% \* 65%) + (50% \* 40%) + (30% \* 75%) = 55.5%*

*The overall margin has declined from 64.5% to 55.5%, a decrease of nine percentage points.*

*Next, let's calculate how much decline is caused by the two drivers we identified in the previous question.*

*The first driver is the decline in margin for services for servers.*

*Decline in overall margin = (20% * 75%) – (20% * 65%) = 2%*

*The second driver is the sales mix change between services for routers and services for switches.*

*Decline in overall margin = [(30% * 40%) + (50% * 75%)] – [(50% * 40%) + (30% * 75%)] = 7%*

*The overall IT services profit margin has declined by nine percentage points, of which seven percentage points are driven by the sales mix change between services for routers and switches. Two percentage points are driven by the decline in the profit margin for services for servers.*

## Question #4

Let's look into why we are selling fewer services for switches. We've pulled together data comparing the prices of Cisco's services for switches with competitor prices. What conclusions can you draw?

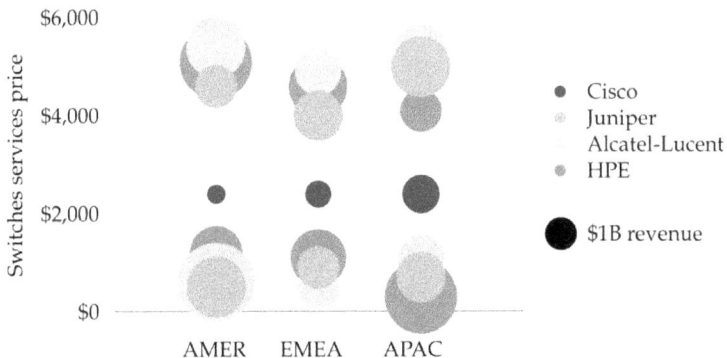

*Solution: There are two key takeaways from this chart.*

*One, competitors vary their prices across geographies while Cisco keeps their prices the same. There is a potential to increase profits if Cisco optimizes its prices across regions.*

*Two, competitors have services for switches that are either priced above $4,000 or below $1,500. This suggests that there is a premium segment and a budget segment. Cisco is getting squeezed out of the market because their prices fall in between.*

*Therefore, Cisco should change their prices such that their services for switches offering is either a premium or budget service. They should also optimize prices across regions to maximize profits.*

## Question #5

We tested how sales quantity would change if we increased the price to make Cisco's services for switches a premium service. Assume costs to deliver the service does not change with price. Based on this information, what price should we set?

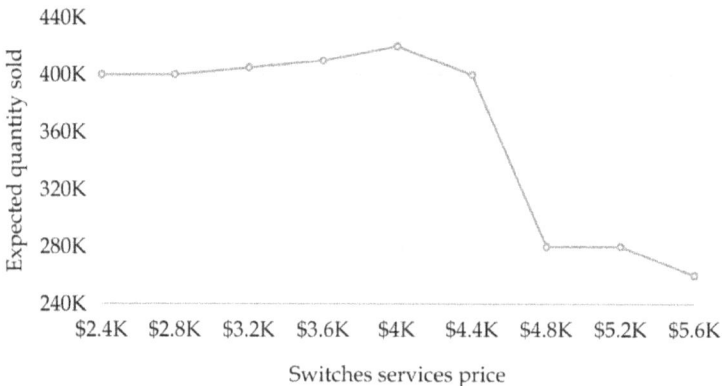

*Solution: We'll look at each price point to determine which one maximizes revenues and profits.*

*From $2,400 to $4,000, price increases while quantity increases. Therefore, the $4,000 price point strictly dominates all points less than it and is one price point we need to calculate revenues for.*

*We'll also need to calculate revenues for a price point of $4,400 because although the price is higher than the previous price point of $4,000, the quantity sold has decreased.*

*Similarly, we'll need to calculate revenues for a price point of $5,200. We don't need to test the price point of $4,800 because the $5,200 price point strictly dominates it since they result in the same quantity sold.*

*Finally, we'll need to test the $5,600 price point since this price is higher than the previous price point of $5,200 but the quantity sold has decreased.*

*If price is set at $4,000, revenue = $4,000 * 420K = $1.68B*

*If price is set at $4,400, revenue = $4,400 * 400K = $1.76B*

*If price is set at $5,200, revenue = $5,200 * 280K = $1.456B*

*If price is set at $5,600, revenue = $5,600 * 260K = $1.456B*

*Therefore, we should price Cisco's services for switches at $4,400.*

## Question #6

Assume that Cisco changes its price for services for switches to $4,400, which results in 400,000 purchases. Costs remain at $600.

Cisco is also considering launching a budget service for switches, priced at $1,500 with a cost of $500. They expect 600,000 purchases, of which 200,000 purchases come from customers switching from purchasing the premium service to the budget service.

Should Cisco launch a budget service for switches?

*Solution: Let's first calculate how much profit Cisco would achieve if they do not launch a budget service for switches.*

*Revenue = 400K * ($4,400 - $600) = $1.52B*

*Next, we'll calculate how much profit Cisco would achieve if it launches a budget service for switches.*

*Revenue = 600K * ($1,500 - $500) + 200K * ($4,400 - $600) = $1.36B*

*Therefore, Cisco should not launch a budget service for switches because sales cannibalization would decrease overall profits from $1.52B to $1.36B.*

## Question #7

Provide a final recommendation based on your work.

*Solution: One recommendation could look like the following:*

*Cisco's IT services business has experienced a decrease in profitability that is mainly driven by the decline in the sales mix of services for switches. I recommend we increase the price of Cisco's services for switches to $4,400 to increase profitability. Three reasons support this.*

*One, competitors are pricing services for switches at either above $4,000 or below $1,500. Cisco's price of $2,400 puts them in between the premium service and budget service segments, squeezing them out of the market.*

*Two, by increasing the price of services for switches to $4,400, Cisco maximizes revenue and profitability. They would sell the same quantity of services for switches but at a much higher price point.*

*Three, we looked into potentially launching a budget service for switches and recommend sticking with just a premium service for switches. A budget service would cannibalize sales of Cisco's premium service, decreasing profits overall.*

*For next steps, I'd look into two areas.*

*One, investigate whether Cisco needs to modify its existing services for switches to justify the increase in price. This will have implications on costs and margins.*

*Two, I'd look into why the margins for services for servers have declined. This is the second driver of the overall decline in profitability.*

# Mini-Cases

# Introduction to Mini-Cases

## What are mini-cases?

Mini-cases ask for a plausible answer or solution to a business question or problem. This might sound similar to a case interview, but there are a few notable differences.

First, mini-cases are much shorter than case interviews. For case interviews, you'll spend 30- to 45-minutes going through seven different steps. For mini-cases, you'll understand the question, ask clarifying questions if needed, structure a framework, and then answer the question.

Second, mini-cases are role-specific. For example, if you are interviewing for a corporate development role, you may be asked to name a company that would be attractive to acquire. If you are interviewing for a product role, you may be asked how you would improve a product.

Case interviews, on the other hand, are focused on more general strategic and operational business problems.

Third, you are assessed more on the content of your answers for mini-cases. You'll need to demonstrate your knowledge of the company, market trends, and other outside information.

Case interviews, on the other hand, are much more focused on the process of how you get the answer. It assesses you more on logic and structured thinking rather than on outside knowledge.

Although mini-cases are quite different from case interviews, you should continue to use logical and structured thinking.

## What are interviewers looking for?

Mini-cases test for four main qualities:

1.  **Business knowledge**: Do you have sufficient knowledge of the company, market trends, and other outside information?

2.  **Business acumen**: Do your ideas and thoughts make sense from a business perspective?

3.  **Logical, structured thinking**: Can you structure your ideas and thoughts logically and clearly?

4.  **Communication skills**: Can you communicate your ideas and thoughts confidently and concisely? Are you easy to understand and follow?

You can improve on the first quality, business knowledge, by conducting thorough company research. Review the "Conducting Company Research" chapter for a refresher on how to research a company effectively.

The more you know about the company, its customers, and its competitors, the more content you have to work with when answering mini-cases.

The second quality, business acumen, can be improved by reading tech articles of business news. The more business news you know, the more different scenarios and situations you will have seen.

When given a mini-case, you can draw upon what you have learned from previous business situations you have read about.

The third and fourth qualities, structured thinking and communication can be improved through practice. Practicing case interviews is a great way to work on creating frameworks and presenting in a clear, concise way. Review the "Case Interview Strategy" chapter for a refresher on these strategies.

# What are the questions I could get asked?

The types of questions you could get asked depend on the role that you are interviewing for. Below are examples of real questions you could get asked for every kind of role.

### Strategy & business operations

- How should Adobe compete in the fragmented micro-stock photography market?

- Which competitors are Cisco's biggest threats?

- What are significant trends impacting eBay?

- What is Expedia's competitive advantage and how sustainable is it?

- What is something that Lyft does better than Uber?

### Product management

- Pick any Amazon product. How would you improve it?

- Design an app for Google's online shopping experience

- What features would you add to Glassdoor?

- How would you redesign Twitter?

- How would you convert Zynga's free customers to paying customers?

## Product marketing

- Amazon is about to release a Kindle Fire for $199 in the lead up to Mother's Day. How would you market it?

- How would you sell the Microsoft Surface tablet to an 80-year-old senior citizen?

- How would you prepare a marketing campaign for Dropbox?

- How can Facebook acquire more users in the younger, upcoming generation?

- How should Instagram encourage more small- and medium-sized businesses to adopt their ad products?

## Business development

- Airbnb is looking to grow their business among university users. Who should they target and how should they do it?

- Name a partnership that you believe has been successful. Why was it successful?

- If Google Chromecast was to do a partnership with T-Mobile, what would that look like?

- For Groupon, are restaurants or retail stores more valuable to partner with?

- What partnership would help Lyft grow its business?

## Corporate development

- What are some different ways to determine the valuation of a company?

- Who should LinkedIn consider acquiring?

- Why do you think Microsoft acquired LinkedIn?

- Which of PayPal's recent acquisitions interests you?

- What factors would you think about when evaluating a private company? How about for a public company?

## Operations

- How should Apple price the new iPhone?

- What do you consider to be the most challenging aspect of Dell's supply chain process?

- For Instacart, how would you improve the shopping process for full-service shoppers?

- For Intel, how would you estimate the capacity required to manufacture a certain number of semiconductor chips before a certain date?

- Is it better for Sony to produce too many or too few PlayStations in the upcoming year?

## Analytics

- Airbnb is launching a new feature, "5-star listing." How would you assess the impact of this new feature?

- Estimate the number of Google searches that are performed each year

- Estimate how many transactions Stripe processes in one day

- How would you measure the value of having one additional driver in Uber's network?

- What metrics would you monitor to detect spam on Quora?

**Finance**

- Name a few financial ratios that can help evaluate a company

- How would you allocate a limited budget across multiple business units?

- How would you improve the profitability of HP's computer and laptop business?

- You are considering shutting down Bing Maps if its projected profitability is too low. What questions would you ask?

- What is important to consider or calculate when deciding on an investment?

## What is the best way to answer mini-cases?

There is a wide variety of questions you could get asked, depending on the type of role you are interviewing for. Due to this, there is no one single strategy for answering all of these questions.

In the upcoming chapters, we'll go through specific strategies to answer the different questions for each role. Each chapter is dedicated to one type of role.

Read through each of the following chapters even if you are not interviewing for that type of role. Tech roles are becoming increasingly cross-functional, so you can never be sure what kinds of questions you could get asked.

For example, some business and corporate development roles could have questions on strategy and business operations. Some product management and marketing roles could have questions on analytics or operations.

Having at least a basic understanding of how to answer questions for all types of roles will make you a well-prepared applicant.

# Summary

- Mini-cases ask for a plausible answer or solution to a business question or problem

- Mini-cases are different from case interviews in that they are shorter, more role-specific, and assess you more on the content of your answer

- Mini-cases test for four main qualities:

    o Business knowledge

    o Business acumen

    o Logical, structured thinking

    o Communication skills

- Have at least a basic understanding of how to answer questions for all types of roles since you can never be sure what types of questions you could get asked

# Mini-Cases for Strategy & Business Operations

## The most common types of questions

To properly answer questions for strategy and business operations roles, you must thoroughly conduct company research. The SWOT analysis will help tremendously. Review the "Conducting Company Research" chapter for a refresher on this.

There are five common types of questions you should prepare for:

1. **Company performance questions**: What is the company's competitive advantage? What is the company doing well and what are they doing poorly?

2. **Growth questions**: How should the company grow? What other markets or customers should the company go after?

3. **Competition questions**: How can the company successfully compete in a particular market? How can the company win over competitors?

4. **Risks and threats questions**: What are the biggest risks or threats to the company?

5. **Trends questions**: What are the major trends impacting the company? How should the company respond to these?

## Company performance questions

Have a perspective on what the company's competitive advantage is. It either comes from having a higher customer willingness to pay or having a lower cost to produce compared to competitors.

There are many reasons why the company may have a higher customer willingness to pay. The product might be superior, the brand name may be worth a premium, or there could be synergies with other products that the customer values.

There are also many different reasons why the company may have a lower cost to produce. The company may have large enough scale to negotiate lower prices with suppliers, the company may have exclusive low-price contracts with suppliers, or the company may have the technical knowledge needed to lower costs.

Knowing the company's competitive advantage will help you identify the company's strengths and weaknesses. Strengths help the company achieve its competitive advantage. Weaknesses put the company's competitive advantage at risk.

**Example**: What is LinkedIn's competitive advantage and how are they performing?

*LinkedIn's competitive advantage lies in its massive user base of over 600 million users. This creates strong network effects that make it difficult for other players to compete.*

*Having more users increases the value of LinkedIn for each user. Users get more value through a more extensive network, better search results, and a larger audience for their posts.*

*Having a massive user base also helps establish LinkedIn as a standard. There are expectations that every working professional has a LinkedIn profile. This increases the stickiness of the platform.*

*In terms of user growth, LinkedIn is performing well because it has become the largest social media platform for professionals. However, in terms of user engagement, there are improvement opportunities.*

*LinkedIn has a low user engagement compared to other major social media networks. We can see the impacts on LinkedIn's monetization because only 20% of users are paying customers. LinkedIn should be achieving higher revenues, given the number of users on its platform.*

*If LinkedIn cannot increase user engagement, it could risk losing users. This jeopardizes their competitive advantage of having network effects due to a massive user base.*

# Growth questions

You should also have a perspective on how the company can grow. When thinking about growth, you can think about growth through organic growth and inorganic growth.

Organic growth is revenue growth that a company achieves through increasing its output and enhancing sales. Inorganic growth is growth through acquisitions or partnerships, which bring in revenue and profit from an external source.

For organic growth, you can think about increasing revenue through existing revenue streams or new revenue streams.

Growth in existing revenue streams includes: changing prices, increasing sales effectiveness, cross-selling, up-selling, entering new geographies, and pursuing new customer segments.

Growth through new revenue streams includes launching new products and launching new services.

For inorganic growth, the company can look at acquiring companies or partnering with companies.

Make sure to consider all of these different avenues for growth when forming a perspective on how the company should grow.

The following framework helps summarize the different opportunities for growth:

- Organic growth

    o Growth through existing revenue streams

        - Changing prices

        - Increasing sales effectiveness

        - Cross-selling

        - Up-selling

        - Entering new geographies

        - Pursuing new customer segments

    o Growth through new revenue streams

        - Launching new products

        - Launching new services

- Inorganic growth

    o Acquiring a company

    o Partnering with a company

**Example**: What are the opportunities for growth for LinkedIn?

*There are a few different attractive opportunities for growth for LinkedIn.*

*One, LinkedIn can consider offering a recruiting-as-a-service package in which LinkedIn recruiters could replace headhunting firms and recruiting departments of companies. Since LinkedIn is the largest professional network, they are in the best position to identify and recruit talented employees for other companies.*

*Two, LinkedIn can continue building out its Learning Solutions platform. As the online learning market continues to grow, LinkedIn can use its data on user skills and company needs to identify critical gaps in employee training. They can then create or acquire content to fill these training gaps and sell the training to companies.*

*Three, LinkedIn can add features to its platform to increase user engagement. As user engagement increases, the value of LinkedIn advertising increases. This will increase customer willingness to pay for LinkedIn's Marketing Solutions.*

*Four, LinkedIn can further monetize existing content. Since only 20% of users are paying customers, LinkedIn can monetize content or features that are currently being offered for free. They can also push for more users to purchase a premium subscription by marketing more aggressively.*

# Competition questions

You should have a viewpoint on how competitors are performing.

The first step is to identify the competitive advantages that other players have. Again, competitive advantage comes from either having a higher customer willingness to pay or having a lower cost to produce compared to other players.

Compare the competitive advantage of the company with the competitive advantages of other players. How can the company sustain its competitive advantage over other players? How can other players maintain their competitive advantage over the company?

Asking yourself these questions will give you an idea of strategic moves that the company needs to make to outcompete other players.

**Example**: How can LinkedIn sustain its competitive advantage over other players?

*There are three major things LinkedIn can do to sustain its competitive advantage over other players.*

*One, LinkedIn should continue to grow its user base. They should focus on targeting more blue-collar workers and working professionals in international countries where LinkedIn has limited penetration.*

*Two, LinkedIn should continue to keep existing users on the platform by identifying features or offerings to increase user engagement. LinkedIn could push curated business news to users. They could also develop a relationship management platform to help professionals keep in touch with former colleagues.*

*Three, LinkedIn should keep an eye on rival professional network platforms. If a competitor starts growing too large or establishing a dominant position in an attractive niche, LinkedIn should consider making acquisitions to build out its network of users further.*

# Risks and threats questions

Next, have a perspective on what the biggest risks and threats to the company are.

Risks can either be internal to the company or external to the company. Internal risks include product risk, team risk, and execution risk. External risks are primarily market risk.

Product risk is the possibility that the product or service will fail to satisfy expectations from customers. Team risk is the possibility that management will be unable to work together effectively. Finally, execution risk is the possibility that the company cannot put its business plans into action.

Market risk is the possibility that regulations, technologies, or customer needs will change. This creates uncertainty that the company has limited control over.

Threats primarily come from competitors. These can either be competitors that have products that directly compete with the company or competitors that have products that are substitutes.

**Example**: What are the biggest risks or threats for LinkedIn?

*There are three significant risks for LinkedIn.*

*One, other large social networks, such as Facebook, may enter the job search and recruiting markets. Facebook has a user base of over two billion people, which poses a serious threat to LinkedIn.*

*Two, as LinkedIn continues to grow, it will have a more difficult time managing fraudulent accounts and spam, which hurts the quality of LinkedIn's platform. LinkedIn must be able to monitor and remove unwanted users and content.*

*Three, user data is increasingly becoming an important issue for social media users. Unfavorable regulations that impact the company's use of customer data could have disastrous effects on some of LinkedIn's premium offerings, such as Talent Solutions.*

# Trends questions

Finally, have a perspective on how major trends are impacting the company and what the company should do in response. Trends that you should consider include customer trends, competitor trends, and market trends.

Customer trends revolve around customer needs, preferences, behaviors, and purchasing habits. How should the company adapt to these changes?

Competitor trends revolve around changes in supplier sourcing, product development, marketing, and overall strategy. What are the actions that competitors are doing that the company should pay attention to?

Market trends revolve around changes in technologies and regulations. What areas should the company invest in due to these market changes?

**Example**: What are the major trends that LinkedIn should be paying attention to?

*There are three meaningful trends that LinkedIn should pay attention to.*

*One, the online learning market is proliferating. Knowledge and skills typically taught in classes or on the job are being digitized into online content that anyone can learn at any time. LinkedIn should look to strengthen its position in this attractive market.*

*Two, there has been a sharp increase in the number of freelance workers and contractors over the past few years. These are jobs that are different from the types of jobs people typically use LinkedIn for. LinkedIn should consider adding features or offerings that cater to this growing segment's needs.*

*Three, an increasing number of companies are using people analytics to analyze employees to improve retention and better attract top talent. Given the amount of employee data that LinkedIn has, there is an opportunity to service this need.*

# Summary

- You should thoroughly conduct company research to answer strategy and business operations questions well

- There are five common types of questions to prepare for:

    o **Company performance questions**: What is the company's competitive advantage? What is the company doing well and what are they doing poorly?

    o **Growth questions**: How should the company grow? What other markets or customers should the company go after?

    o **Competition questions**: How can the company successfully compete in a particular market? How can the company win over competitors?

    o **Risks and threats questions**: What are the biggest risks or threats to the company?

    o **Trends questions**: What are the major trends impacting the company? How should the company respond to these?

- A company's competitive advantage comes from having a higher customer willingness to pay or from having a lower cost to produce compared to competitors

- Growth is either organic growth or inorganic growth

    o Organic growth includes increasing revenue from existing revenue streams

        ▪ Growth through existing revenue streams includes changing prices, increasing sales effectiveness, cross-selling, up-selling, entering new geographies, and pursuing new customer segments

- Growth through new revenue streams includes launching new products and launching new services

  o Inorganic growth includes acquiring companies and partnering with companies

- Internal risks include product risk, team risk, and execution risk while external risks are primarily market risk

- Threats include competitors and substitutes

- Trends can be categorized as customer trends, competitor trends, and market trends

# Practice

For the company you are interviewing with:

1. What are they doing well and what are they doing poorly?

2. What are the most attractive opportunities for growth?

3. What is something that competitors are doing better?

4. What are their biggest threats?

5. What are the major trends impacting their business?

# Mini-Cases for Product Management & Marketing

## The most common types of questions

There is meaningful overlap between product management and product marketing roles. So, the questions for these two roles are combined in this chapter.

In preparing for product questions, know the following about the products of the company you are interviewing with:

- Who are the customers of these products?

- What pain points do these products solve for?

- How have these products changed over time?

- How do these products compare to products of competitors?

Knowing these answers will help you form a strong foundation for answering product questions. It will be tough to answer product questions if you aren't familiar with the company's products.

Also, familiarize yourself with a few products outside of the company that you are interviewing for. Sometimes, interviewers will let you choose your favorite product to discuss.

There are two common product questions you will likely be asked:

1.  How would you improve or design a particular product?

2.  How would you market a specific product?

For each of these questions, we'll provide a structured framework to help you develop a thoughtful answer.

## Product improvement and design questions

When asked how you would improve or design a product, resist the urge to list the first few ideas that come to your head. Instead, follow this systematic approach to demonstrate to the interviewer how you think about the product improvement and design process.

There are five main steps:

1.  Identify a customer segment to target

2.  Select a pain point to focus on

3.  Brainstorm product improvements or designs

4.  Assess which idea is best

5.  Explain how you would test this

**Identify a customer segment to target**

The goal of the first step is to focus and narrow down the scope of product improvement or design to one specific customer segment.

There are two reasons why you should do this.

One, customers can have a wide range of needs and preferences. Trying to improve or design a product that would benefit every single customer can be very challenging.

Two, by focusing on a specific customer segment, you can develop product improvements and designs that are more specific and tailored to the segment's needs. You will avoid suggesting product ideas that are generic and not impactful.

Therefore, start by listing the different customer segments that come to mind. Select one segment and provide a reason why you are focusing on that segment.

You might choose a segment because they are the largest segment or you might pick a segment if their needs are underserved.

**Select a pain point to focus on**

Brainstorm a list of pain points for the selected customer segment. These can be unmet customer needs or features of the product that customers find frustrating, time-consuming, or difficult to use.

Select one pain point and provide a reason why you are focusing on it. You might select a pain point if it is the most common, the most severe, or the most practical to solve for.

**Brainstorm product improvements or designs**

Now that you have chosen a pain point to focus on, brainstorm a list of different ways to solve for that pain point.

Try to have 3 – 5 different ideas. Include a few ideas that are creative and unconventional. This demonstrates originality and out-of-the-box thinking.

**Assess which idea is best**

For this step, create a list of criteria to assess your different ideas. Common criteria include:

- Number of users affected

- Magnitude of impact

- User experience

- Cost

- Ease of implementation

Select the most important criteria based on the nature of the product and the pain point. Afterward, assess each of your product ideas based on the list of criteria you have developed.

You can assess your ideas either quantitatively or qualitatively.

The most common way to quantitatively score ideas is to give them one, two, or three points for each criterion. The idea that has the highest total number of points will be chosen.

Some criteria may be significantly more important than others. In this case, you can consider weighting the point values differently. For example, if the magnitude of impact is by far the most essential criterion, you can double the point value. Each idea will be given two, four, or six points for this criterion.

In assessing your ideas qualitatively, talk through how each idea performs on the criteria you have selected. Choose the improvement or design that has the most positive assessment overall.

**Explain how you would test this**

After you have selected your best idea, suggest how you would test whether this product improvement or design works. Specify what metrics you would want to measure to determine this.

This step is not always necessary, but it demonstrates to the interviewer that you can think like a product manager. Product roles involve a lot of testing and iterating on features and improvements.

A/B testing is the most common way to test a new product feature or design. In A/B testing, you compare the performance of two variations of a product against one another.

Typically, you would run an experiment in which one group of customers is given the original or older product and another group of customers is given the new and improved product.

After defining the right metrics to measure performance, you can determine which version of the product performs better.

# Example of a product improvement question

Now that you understand the five steps to answering product improvement or design questions, let's take a look at an example.

**Example**: How would you improve YouTube?

*For this question, I'll assume that the goal of the improvement is to increase user engagement on the platform, which can be measured as the amount of time a user spends on YouTube.*

*First, I'll think through the different customer segments and pick one to focus on. Three customer segments immediately come to mind:*

- *Entertainment seekers are users that are bored who are looking for interesting videos to watch to pass the time*

- *Information seekers are users looking to learn a new skill or acquire information on a topic*

- *Music seekers are users looking for background music or sounds to play while they are doing something else*

*Out of these segments, I will focus on entertainment seekers because this segment probably makes up the most significant proportion of YouTube's user base.*

*Next, I'll identify a pain point to focus on. Entertainment seekers have a few different pain points:*

- *The discovery process they go through to find entertaining videos takes time and effort*

- *Entertainment seekers find long videos dull and too slow to watch*

- *They get irritated when videos have clickbait titles that do not live up to expectations.*

*Among these pain points, I'm going to focus on the tedious video discovery process because it is probably the biggest pain point for these users.*

*Now, I will brainstorm a few ideas on how to make the video discovery process easier.*

- *YouTube could recommend videos based on videos that friends have seen. Since friends tend to have similar interests and tastes, these videos will likely be entertaining to entertainment seekers*

- *YouTube can have a continuous, curated video feed such that users do not have to search for the next video. Users can click on a skip button to immediately jump into the following video, which will be curated by an algorithm based on video history*

- *YouTube could send a curated playlist to the user each day. These videos would be selected by an algorithm based on video history*

*I will assess each of these ideas on impact, user experience, and ease of implementation.*

*The first idea, recommending videos based on videos that friends have seen, would have minimal impact if the user does not have friends that use YouTube frequently.*

*Additionally, this idea does not change the user experience much because entertainment seekers would still need to decide whether to watch a recommended video. The upside of this idea is that it would not be difficult to implement.*

*The second idea, having a continuous, curated video feed, could have a tremendous impact. It removes the burden of decision-making from entertainment seekers because YouTube videos are automatically played.*

*The user experience is also an improvement because the user only needs to click a skip button when they are bored. The downside of this idea is that developing a good algorithm could require substantial investment.*

*The third idea, sending a curated playlist to the user each day, would have some impact on users. The decision making process is slightly simplified because the user receives a shorter list of videos to choose from. However, once the playlist is finished, the user would still need to look for more videos on their own.*

*Additionally, the user experience is not ideal. Getting an email or notification every day can be annoying. The upside of this idea is that it is the most straightforward to implement.*

*Based on my assessment, the continuous, curated video feed seems to be the most promising.*

*To test this idea, I would develop a minimal viable product and use A/B testing to assess the performance of this feature.*

*One customer group would be given access to this feature while another customer group would not. I would measure the difference in minutes of video consumption between the two groups for one month to determine if user engagement has increased.*

## Product marketing questions

Product marketing questions typically ask you to develop a plan or strategy to market and sell a particular product. For these questions, resist the urge to list the first few ideas that come to your head.

Instead, follow a systematic approach to demonstrate to the interviewer that you can think about product marketing in a strategic and structured way. There are two frameworks you can use to help you answer these questions:

1. STP

2. 4 P's

STP stands for segmentation, targeting, and positioning. To develop a marketing strategy, use this framework to identify a customer segment and positioning statement for your product.

## Segmentation

The first step is to understand how the market is segmented. Customers have a wide variety of needs and preferences. Therefore, a broad marketing strategy targeting every customer will not be as effective as a tailored marketing strategy focused on a specific customer segment.

You will need to decide what type of segmentation makes the most sense for your product. You can segment customers on needs, use cases, or various demographics, such as age, geography, income, lifestyle, and attitudes.

*Example*: *If you are marketing a social media platform, it may make sense to segment customers by age. If you are selling a laptop, it may make sense to segment customers by use case. If you are selling enterprise software, you might segment by business size.*

At the end of this step, you should have a list of the different customer segments.

## Targeting

The next step is to evaluate the attractiveness of each segment and choose a target segment to focus on. There are many different factors to consider when selecting a target segment:

- Which segment is the largest?

- Which segment is growing the quickest?

- What segment is the most profitable?

- Which segment is the most accessible?

- Which segment is the best fit for your product?

- Which segment has the potential for the most improvement?

- Which segment is the most influenced by marketing?

Once you have selected a customer segment to focus on, you can move onto the next step, developing a positioning statement.

## Positioning

Now, you will determine how to position and communicate the product to potential customers.

Your positioning and communication of the product should be tailored to the specific needs and preferences of the customer segment you have decided to focus on. In determining how to position the product, ask yourself the following questions:

- What makes this customer segment different from others?

- What does this customer segment value?

- What are the attitudes or beliefs of this customer segment?

Below are a few examples of positioning statements from well-known companies:

- **Amazon**: For customers who want to purchase a wide variety of products online, Amazon offers a one-stop shopping experience

- **Apple**: For technology users who want a seamless experience, Apple leads the industry with the most innovative and easy-to-use products

- **Disney**: For consumers looking for unique entertainment, Disney provides magical memories and experiences

Having a positioning statement will help you decide the best way to market the product. To do that, you will move onto the next framework, the 4 P's.

The 4 P's stands for product, place, promotion, and price. The goal of 4 P's is to determine the best way to market the product.

## Product

If there are multiple products or different versions of a product, you will need to decide which product to market. To do this, you will need to fully understand the benefits and points of differentiation of each product.

Select the product that best fits customer needs and the positioning statement you developed for the segment you are focusing on.

## Place

You will need to decide where the product will be sold to customers. Different customer segments have different purchasing habits and behaviors. Therefore, some distribution channels will be more effective than others.

Should the product be sold directly to the customer online? Should the product be sold in the company's stores? Should the product be sold through retail partners instead?

## Promotion

You will need to decide how to spread information about the product to customers. Different customer segments have different media consumption habits and preferences. Therefore, some promotional strategies will be more effective than others.

Promotional techniques and strategies include advertising, social media marketing, email marketing, search engine marketing, video marketing, and public relations. Select the strategies and techniques that will be the most effective.

## Price

You will need to decide how to price the product. Pricing is important because it determines the profits and the quantity of units sold. Pricing can also communicate information on the quality or value of the product.

If you price the product too high, you may be pricing the product above your customer segment's willingness to pay. This would lead to lost sales.

If you price the product too low, you may be losing potential profit from customers who were willing to pay a higher price. You may also be losing profits from customers who perceive the product as low-quality due to a low price point.

In deciding on a price, you can consider the costs to produce the product, the prices of other similar products, and the value that you are providing to customers.

# Example of a product marketing question

Let's take a look at an example question to illustrate how you can use the STP and 4 P's framework.

**Example**: How would you sell the Microsoft Surface tablet to an 80-year-old senior citizen?

*First, I'll identify the distinguishing attributes of this segment to develop a positioning statement for the product. Some characteristics of senior citizens are that they:*

- *Value keeping in touch with family*

- *Have a lot of free time because they are retired*

- *Watch television and read newspapers*

- *Find technology challenging to use*

*From this, I propose the following positioning statement:*

*For senior citizens looking to connect and stay close to family members, the Microsoft Surface tablet is an easy way to bring families together.*

*Senior citizens do not have a tremendous amount of money to spend, so it probably makes sense to sell them a basic version of the Microsoft Surface tablet. They do not need additional storage or high-performance upgrades.*

*Moving onto the marketing strategy, Microsoft should advertise on television, running ads that show senior citizens using the tablet to video chat with their grandchildren. Microsoft should run these ads during the late afternoon or early evening, when most senior citizens watch television.*

*For distribution, senior citizens typically do not make purchases online. It can also be difficult for them to go to retail stores because of their age and limited transportation options.*

*Therefore, the ads should provide a phone number for senior citizens to call to make their purchases. The product will be delivered directly to their front doorsteps to reduce any friction in purchasing.*

*For pricing, Microsoft should advertise the lower price of a basic tablet model to increase the likelihood that senior citizens will make a purchase.*

*At a high-level, this is the marketing strategy I would use to sell the Microsoft Surface tablet to an 80-year-old citizen.*

# Summary

- There are two common product questions:

    o How would you improve or design a product?

    o How would you market a specific product?

- There are five main steps in answering product improvement and design questions

    o Identify a customer segment to target

    o Select a pain point to focus on

    o Brainstorm product improvements or designs

    o Assess which idea is best

    o Explain how you would test this

- For product marketing questions that ask you to develop a marketing plan or strategy, use the STP and 4 P's framework

    o **Segmentation**: Create a list of customer segments

    o **Targeting**: Select one segment to focus on

    o **Positioning**: Decide how to position and communicate the product

    o **Product**: Decide which product or version of the product to market

    o **Place**: Decide where the product will be sold

    o **Promotion**: Decide how to spread information about the product to customers

    o **Price**: Decide how to price the product

# Practice

1.  How would you improve the iPhone?

    *First, let's identify the different customer segments and select one to focus on. There are a few different customer segments that come to mind:*

    - *Entertainment users: This segment uses the iPhone for gaming, videos, and music*

    - *Photography users: This segment uses the iPhone for taking pictures and posting to social media*

    - *Productivity users: This segment uses the iPhone to handle emails, calendar events, and planning*

    *I'd like to focus on photography users because almost everyone uses their iPhone's camera as their primary camera for day-to-day picture taking.*

    *There are many pain points with taking and managing photos on the iPhone:*

    - *There is poor image quality if there is not enough light while taking a picture*

    - *It is difficult to clearly capture far away objects using the iPhone's camera*

    - *Selfies are annoying to take due to the location of the button that takes photos*

    - *Photos take up a lot of space, so not all of them can be kept on the iPhone*

    - *It is time-consuming and tedious to manage all of the photos that are taken*

*I'd like to focus on the last pain point because it is a pain point I experience. After taking photos, it is time-consuming to look through all of the pictures to decide which ones to keep or delete.*

*Next, I'll brainstorm a few ways to address this pain point:*

- *The iPhone could be configured to take multiple pictures over one to three seconds and save only the best image*

- *Photos are taken as usual, but the iPhone will make recommendations on what photos to delete when the user browses their photo album*

- *Photos are taken as usual, but there will be a feature added in which the iPhone highlights the best photos when the user browsers their photo album*

*I will assess each idea based on impact, user experience, and ease of implementation.*

*The first idea is very impactful since it automatically chooses and keeps the best photos. However, it can be a poor user experience because what the user sees on the camera may not be the photo that is taken.*

*Additionally, developing an algorithm that decides which photo is best will be difficult without large quantities of validated data.*

*The second idea is moderately impactful because it saves users some time. The user experience is excellent because the iPhone provides unprompted recommendations on photos to delete, but the user has ultimate decision rights.*

*Developing the algorithm for this feature will be easier than developing the algorithm for the first idea. It is easier to identify a bad photo than it is to identify a good photo. For poor photos, the algorithm could focus mainly on blurriness, closed eyes, and insufficient lighting.*

*The third idea is also moderately impactful in saving the user time. The user experience is great because it involves minimal effort from the user to see a curated collection of the best photos. However, developing an algorithm that selects good photos is likely difficult.*

*Therefore, I recommend that we improve the iPhone by adding a feature that suggests which pictures should be deleted.*

*We can test this feature through A/B testing. One group of users would have access to this feature while another group would not. We can measure differences in the amount of time spent browsing through photos to see if the added feature performs well.*

2.  How would you market Instagram to small- and medium-sized businesses?

    *I'll first identify the characteristics of this customer segment. These businesses typically:*

    - *Don't have much money to spend on marketing*

    - *Don't have a full-time employee for social media*

    - *Value having a personal touch with customers*

    - *Have difficulty competing against larger businesses*

    *Based on these characteristics, one potential positioning statement is the following:*

    *For businesses that want to stay in touch with customers, but have a limited budget, Instagram is a powerful, low-maintenance platform to develop meaningful relationships with customers.*

    *Moving onto marketing strategy, we want to market a business Instagram account.*

    *We should price the product as free because small- and medium-sized businesses have limited budgets. We may even want to offer them free credit for Instagram advertising.*

*Once these businesses have used the platform and see Instagram's value, they can be convinced to spend money on Instagram's premium offerings.*

*We do not want larger businesses to take advantage of these free offerings because they have money to spend.*

*Therefore, digital marketing is likely the most effective channel. Through online ads, we can specifically target small- and medium-sized businesses and avoid targeting larger companies.*

3. For the company you are interviewing with, pick one product or service. How would you improve it?

4. For the company you are interviewing with, pick one product or service. What customer segment would you target and how would you market to them?

# Mini-Cases for Business & Corporate Development

## The most common types of questions

There is meaningful overlap between business development and corporate development roles, so the mini-cases for these roles are combined in this chapter.

Three questions are frequently asked:

1. What company should we potentially acquire?

2. How would you determine the valuation of a company?

3. What company should we partner with?

In preparing for these roles, you should be familiar with the recent acquisitions and partnerships the company has made. It will be difficult to suggest companies to acquire or partner with if you do not know what has been done already.

In this chapter, we'll go through each of these questions and provide strategies and frameworks to help you develop a thoughtful answer.

# Potential acquisition questions

To answer these types of questions, become familiar with the different motivations for making an acquisition. Each motivation has a different goal that the company is trying to achieve.

Reasons why a company would make an acquisition:

- Remove a competitor from the market

- Acquire talent

- Acquire intellectual property, proprietary technology, or a brand's name

- Gain access to the target's customers

- Gain access to the target's distribution channels

- Diversify its product portfolio

- Realize cost synergies

Before brainstorming potential companies, decide what the goals of the acquisition are. Then, brainstorm and research a list of companies to evaluate.

A company is an attractive acquisition target if it:

- Competes in attractive markets

- Performs well financially

- Has a meaningful market share

- Has customers and distribution channels that can be leveraged to increase revenues

- Has proprietary processes or technologies that lead the industry

- Has products or services that cannot be developed internally

- Has talented employees that cannot be found elsewhere

- Has many costs that can be consolidated after the acquisition

- Has an acquisition price that is affordable

The qualities that you assess potential acquisition targets on will vary depending on the goal of the acquisition. Select the acquisition target that is the most attractive based on your assessment.

Finally, structure your answer. Start by stating which company you believe is an attractive acquisition target. Then, provide at least three reasons that support your choice.

Let's look at an example of an answer to an acquisition question.

**Example**: What is a potential company that LinkedIn should consider acquiring?

*LinkedIn should consider acquiring UpWork, a website to find and hire freelancers. There are three reasons LinkedIn should make this acquisition.*

*One, this would enable LinkedIn to be a full-suite platform for hiring both temporary and permanent employees. Currently, most of LinkedIn's users are permanent employees and LinkedIn is used for full-time hiring. In contrast, Upwork consists entirely of freelancers, making them a valuable complementary network to incorporate into LinkedIn.*

*Two, an acquisition of UpWork would enable cross-selling opportunities. LinkedIn could sell learning or training modules to Upwork freelancers to make them more hirable. LinkedIn could also sell its premium offerings, such as Marketing Solutions or Talent Solutions, to Upwork's clients.*

*Three, UpWork is a financially attractive company. They are one of the leading freelancing companies with over ten million users and five million*

*clients. They are performing well financially, with revenue growing at 15%*
*per year and their gross margins are over 70%.*

# Valuation questions

You may be asked how you would determine the valuation of a
private or public company. While there are many ways to do this,
you should be familiar with the following six major methods.

**Market capitalization**: This method determines a company's
valuation by multiplying the company's share price by the total
number of shares outstanding.

**Discounted Cash Flow (DCF)**: First, forecast all future cash flows of
the company. Then, discount all cash flows to the present day using
the company's discount rate. The resulting net present value is the
company's valuation.

**Comparable companies' multiples**: This method uses the metrics of
other similarly sized businesses in the same industry to determine a
valuation. The two most common metrics used are the P/E ratio and
the EV/EBITDA multiple.

The P/E ratio stands for price to earnings. It measures a company's
current share price relative to its earnings per share.

The EV/EBITDA ratio stands for enterprise value to earnings before
interest, taxes, depreciation, and amortization. It measures the
company's total value relative to a measure of the company's cash
earnings in one year.

If you know the P/E or EV/EBITDA ratio of other similar
companies, you can use these ratios to determine the valuation.

**Cost approach**: This method values the company by estimating the
cost it would take to build the company from nothing.

**Book value**: This method values the company by the value of shareholder's equity on the balance sheet. This can be calculated by subtracting total liabilities from total assets.

**Liquidation value**: This method values a company by determining the cash that the company would receive if it liquidated all of its assets and paid off all of its liabilities.

Let's take a look at an example of a valuation question.

**Example**: How would you determine the valuation of a small, private company that has generated no revenues yet?

*There are two different ways we can determine the company's valuation.*

*One, we can use a cost approach to estimate how much it would cost to build the company from nothing. The total estimated cost would be the valuation of the company.*

*Two, we can estimate the company's liquidation value, which is the amount of cash the company would receive if it sold all of its assets and paid off all of its liabilities.*

# Potential partnership questions

Similar to acquisition questions, become familiar with the different reasons why a company would form a partnership.

Reasons why a company would form a partnership:

- Build brand awareness

- Attract new customers

- Expand market coverage

- Broaden product and service offerings

- Generate economies of scale

- Overcome other competition in the market

- Share knowledge or resources

- Share business risks

Before brainstorming potential companies, decide what the goals of the partnership are. Then, brainstorm and research a list of companies to evaluate.

A company is attractive to partner with if it:

- Has high brand awareness

- Provides access to attractive markets or geographies

- Has complementary customers or distribution channels

- Has complementary products or services

- Has knowledge or resources that are useful to share

- Is financially stable enough to deliver in the partnership

The qualities that you assess potential partnerships on will vary depending on what the goal is. Select the company that is the most attractive based on your assessment.

As always, structure your answer. Start by stating which company you believe would be an excellent company to partner with. Then, provide at least three reasons that support this.

Let's look at an example of an answer to a partnership question.

**Example**: What is a potential partnership that LinkedIn should consider forming?

*LinkedIn should partner with prominent universities, such as Harvard, Stanford, and MIT, to grow their online learning business. There are four reasons that support this.*

*One, the online learning market is growing tremendously. LinkedIn already sells recruiting tools, so employee learning and development tools are a promising adjacent market to enter. This partnership with universities would enable LinkedIn to offer an end-to-end recruiting solution to help companies identify, hire, and train employees.*

*Two, the prestigious brand names of top universities would add credibility to LinkedIn's learning and development offerings. This will help LinkedIn attract customers toward their Learning Solutions platform.*

*Three, top universities also typically have the leading thought leaders. This ensures that there will be high-quality content to keep customers satisfied.*

*Four, the partnership makes sense for universities because LinkedIn has the most amount of data on employee knowledge and skill gaps. This will help universities produce the most relevant learning modules that will bring meaningful additional revenue.*

# Summary

- Three questions are frequently asked:

    o What company should we potentially acquire?

    o How would you determine the valuation of a company?

    o What company should we partner with?

- To answer potential acquisition questions, state which company you believe is an attractive acquisition target and then provide at least three reasons that support this

- There are many reasons for making an acquisition:

    o Remove a competitor from the market

    o Acquire talent

    o Acquire intellectual property, proprietary technology, or a brand's name

    o Gain access to the target's customers

    o Gain access to the target's distribution channels

    o Diversify its product portfolio

    o Realize cost synergies

- A company is an attractive acquisition target if it:

    o Competes in attractive markets

    o Performs well financially

    o Has a meaningful market share

- o Has customers and distribution channels that can be leveraged to increase revenues

- o Has proprietary processes or technologies

- o Has products that cannot be developed internally

- o Has talented employees

- o Has many costs that can be consolidated

- o Has an acquisition price that is affordable

- There are six major ways to value a company

    - o Market capitalization

    - o Discounted cash flow (DCF)

    - o Comparable companies' multiples

    - o Cost approach

    - o Book value

    - o Liquidation value

- To answer potential partnership questions, state which company you believe would be a great company to partner with and then provide at least three reasons that support this

- There are many reasons for forming a partnership:

    - o Build brand awareness

    - o Attract new customers

    - o Expand market coverage

    - o Broaden product and service offerings

- o   Generate economies of scale

- o   Overcome other competition in the market

- o   Share knowledge or resources

- o   Share business risks

- A company is attractive to partner with if it:

  - o   Has high brand awareness

  - o   Provides access to attractive markets or geographies

  - o   Has complementary distribution channels

  - o   Has complementary products or services

  - o   Has knowledge or resources that are useful to share

  - o   Is financially stable enough to deliver value

# Practice

For the company you are interviewing with:

1. What is a company or organization that the company should partner with?

2. What is an attractive potential acquisition target?

3. For your proposed acquisition target, how would you determine the valuation of that company?

# Mini-Cases for Operations

## The most common types of questions

While strategy focuses on defining where the company should play and what they should do to win, operations focuses on how to get things done smoothly and efficiently.

Questions for operations roles will focus on assessing how you would run and execute the day-to-day business of the organization. Operations revolve around answering the question of "how?"

- How should we source the materials and labor needed for our product?

- How do we produce our product?

- How do we manage inventory of our product?

- How do we sell our product to customers?

- How do we distribute our product?

- How do we handle customer service?

There are three major types of questions:

- Process improvement questions

- Pricing questions

- Forecasting and capacity planning questions

Let's take a look at each question type to learn an effective approach to deliver an outstanding answer.

## Process improvement questions

Process improvement questions assess your ability to break down a process to identify opportunities for improvement.

There are four main steps to answering these questions:

1. Identify the most important performance metrics

2. Decompose the process into separate, distinct components

3. Use the PPT framework to assess the people, process, and technology for each component

4. Prioritize the most important improvements

For the first step, decide or clarify with the interviewer what the performance metric of success is. Improving a process can mean many things, such as increasing throughput, quality, or efficiency.

The second step is to break down the overall process into separate, distinct components. You will have to use your judgment and discretion to decide the best way to decompose the process.

A helpful way to think about components is to think about inputs and outputs. Each component has something that it is given, which is the input. From this, an action is performed to convert this to something else, which is the output.

*Example*: *Let's say that you are looking to improve how Amazon fulfills orders to customers to decrease delivery time. You might decompose the process into the following components:*

- *Take the customer order information from the website*

- *Determine the right warehouses to ship from*

- *Select and package the right products*

- *Ship the products to large distribution centers*

- *Determine which local delivery vehicle and route the products should be transported in*

- *Deliver the products to the customer's doorstep*

*Let's take a look at one component. In selecting and packaging the right products, the input is a warehouse worker receiving a list of customer order items. The output is a box of products that is ready to be shipped.*

The third step is to assess the people, process, and technology for each component. This is known as the PPT framework.

**People**: Do you have enough people in place? Do people have the right backgrounds and experiences? Are people properly trained and prepared? Are people being managed and motivated properly?

**Process**: Are the right series of steps being performed? Should certain steps be added? Should others be removed?

**Technology**: Is technology being used? Are the right technologies being used effectively?

*Example*: *Let's return to the previous Amazon example. We will assess the component in which a warehouse worker receives a list of items from a customer order and is tasked with selecting and packaging the right products to be shipped.*

*Let's analyze people first.*

*Overall, the right people are in place. The job of selecting and packaging products does not require technical expertise or high education. Amazon provides sufficient training to workers. Workers also receive bonuses based on their efficiency, so they are properly motivated.*

*Next, we'll analyze the process.*

*There are some opportunities to improve the process in which warehouse workers select and package products. Currently, workers are given one customer order list at a time.*

*Speed could be improved if warehouse workers received multiple customer order lists instead. This would decrease the number of warehouse trips workers would need to make. However, this would also increase the risk of packaging the wrong customer products together.*

*Finally, we'll analyze technology.*

*Some technology is used. For each order, warehouse workers are given the best route to take in selecting and picking up products in the warehouse.*

*However, the act of selecting and picking up products is very labor-intensive. There is an opportunity to use automated robots, which can move much faster than humans, to choose and pick up products in the warehouse.*

For the fourth and final step, you will prioritize the most important improvements. Which improvements best improve the performance metric of success?

**Example**: *Continuing with the Amazon example, the most impactful improvement identified so far is using automated robots to select and package the right products. This would remove manual labor and make the process of choosing and packaging products fully automated.*

# Pricing questions

Pricing questions will ask you to walk the interviewer through how you would price a particular product or service. To answer these types of questions, know the different pricing strategies.

There are three main pricing strategies. Your answer to pricing questions will likely be a mix of these:

- Pricing based on costs

- Pricing based on competition

- Pricing based on value added

## Pricing based on costs

The first pricing strategy is to apply a profit margin on the total costs to produce or deliver the product or service.

*Example: If you are selling a laptop that costs $400 to produce and want a profit margin of 25%, price the laptop at $500.*

Pricing based on costs helps you determine the minimum price you should set the product at. It typically does not make sense to price a product below the total costs to produce that product.

Pricing based on costs also helps you avoid decreasing the company's overall profit margins.

*Example: Let's say that the laptop company had an overall profit margin of 30%. Given this, you know that pricing the laptop at $500 would decrease the company's overall margins since the new laptop has a 25% margin. Therefore, the price of the new laptop would need to be at least $520 to maintain an overall company profit margin of 30%.*

## Pricing based on competition

The second pricing strategy is to price based on what competitors are charging for products similar to yours. This pricing strategy helps you get a sense of the potential price range of your product.

*Example: Let's say that your company's laptop has 32GB of RAM and a quad-core processor. For computers, more RAM and more cores typically mean better performance.*

*One competitor sells a laptop with 16GB of RAM and a dual-core processor for $600. Another competitor sells a laptop with 64GB of RAM and an eight-core processor for $1,500.*

*Given this, the range of possible prices for your laptop is $600 - $1,500. You'll be unlikely to sell your laptop for more than $1,500 because customers could get a better performing laptop for $1,500. Similarly, you would not want to sell your laptop for less than $600 because your laptop is better than a competitor's $600 laptop.*

**Pricing based on value added**

The third pricing strategy is pricing based on value added. This strategy determines price by quantifying the benefits that the product provides customers.

***Example***: *Let's say that you sell laptops that have a proprietary processor that is guaranteed to work for three years. Other laptops in the market require about $50 per year in maintenance to function correctly.*

*The benefit you are providing the customer is a more reliable laptop. This reduces the need for customers to spend money on maintenance. The proprietary processor saves the customer $50 per year in maintenance for three years, which is a $150 savings.*

*Therefore, you could price your laptop up to $150 more than that of competitors based on the value you are providing to customers.*

# Forecasting and capacity planning questions

Forecasting is the process of making predictions based on existing data. The most common forecasting problem in business is predicting customer demand for your product to have the right level of inventory and production capacity.

To answer these questions, you should understand two things. One, you should know the three different ways of forecasting. Two, you should understand the inventory trade-offs between overstocking and understocking.

We'll first discuss the three different ways of forecasting:

- Qualitative techniques

- Time series analysis and projection

- Causal models

## Qualitative techniques

The first type of forecasting, qualitative techniques, is most commonly used when data is scarce. You would use this method to forecast customer demand for a new kind of product that has never been launched before.

Qualitative techniques can be conducted by interviewing experts and visionaries in the field, conducting consumer and market research, or by analyzing the growth of similar new products.

*Example: Let's say that Google launches augmented reality contact lenses that allow the user to see notifications, such as text messages and news, right in their eyes. They are trying to predict how many pairs of contact lenses they would sell in the first few years.*

*Since this is a new product, there is no historical data to look at. To forecast demand, you can conduct interviews with tech experts and run consumer surveys. You could also look at the past adoption of other disruptive technologies, such as the smartphone or tablet, to make a prediction.*

## Time series analysis and projection

The second type of forecasting is a time series analysis. This is most commonly used when several years of data for a product is available and when trends are relatively stable.

Time series analysis focuses on analyzing historical data to identify patterns and pattern changes. Time series analysis can predict seasonality or cyclicality in customer demand. There are many different ways to do a time series analysis, such as taking a moving average or exponential smoothing.

*Example*: *If Apple is forecasting demand for its AirPods for the third quarter, there are many years of historical data on sales. Apple could look at third quarter AirPods sales over the last few years to see the trend in sales and make predictions for the upcoming third quarter.*

## Causal models

The third type of forecasting is using a causal model. These models are used when historical data is available and enough analysis has been performed to identify how different factors impact the forecast.

Causal models are complex and may incorporate the results of a time series analysis. An example of a type of causal model is a multiple regression model, which uses the values of different variables to predict an outcome.

*Example*: *Airbnb is predicting how many nights customers will book on their platform in December. Airbnb has a tremendous amount of data on how seasonality, the number of listings on the platform, and price, impact the number of bookings. Airbnb could use a multiple regression model based on these factors to predict the number of nights booked in December.*

## Inventory trade-offs

Now that you understand the different ways of forecasting, we'll discuss inventory trade-offs. Companies are always making trade-offs between carrying too much inventory and carrying too little.

The primary advantage of carrying too much inventory is that the company can meet customer demand if it is higher than expected.

There are several disadvantages to this. If customer demand is lower than expected, the company will be holding onto inventory that it cannot sell. This is costly because unsold products take up space in warehouses. These costs are known as storage costs.

Additionally, as time goes on, the company's inventory may begin becoming obsolete. New products and technologies may make the company's leftover products no longer desirable. As a result, companies may need to sell leftover products at a steep discount to clear their inventory.

The primary advantage of carrying too little inventory is that the company will not have leftover products. The company can ensure that none of the products they sell will need to be discounted and sold at a loss.

There are several disadvantages to this. If demand is higher than expected, not all customers will be able to purchase the company's product. These are lost sales for the company.

Additionally, this can lead to a poor customer experience and unhappy customers. Some customers may even decide to purchase a similar product from a competitor. By having insufficient inventory, companies allow competitors to take customers and market share away from them.

Ultimately, the decision on how much inventory to carry depends on the overage and underage costs.

The overage cost is the cost of storage of unsold inventory and the loss in profit from discounting unsold inventory. The underage cost is the cost of lost sales and the cost of having unsatisfied customers who may not purchase from you in the future.

If overage costs are higher than underage costs, the company should stock inventory at a lower level than expected demand. If underage costs are higher than overage costs, the company should carry more inventory than anticipated demand.

If you know the exact overage costs and underage costs, you can calculate the precise inventory level you should carry using the newsvendor model, which is a core concept in supply chain and inventory management.

While you may not directly be asked to perform calculations using the newsvendor model in an interview, you should at least be familiar with how the model works.

We'll illustrate the newsvendor model in the following example.

**Example**: A newsvendor buys newspapers in bulk for $0.50 each and sells them for $2.50. Unsold newspapers are thrown away at the end of the day.

If the daily demand for newspapers is normally distributed with a mean of 100 newspapers and a standard deviation of 20, how many newspapers should the newsvendor carry each day?

*To determine the optimal inventory level, we'll first calculate the underage and overage costs.*

*The underage cost is a lost newspaper sale. The newsvendor loses $2 in profit for each customer that they turn away due to insufficient inventory.*

*The overage cost is the cost of throwing out a newspaper. For each unsold newspaper, the newsvendor does not recoup the $0.50 that was paid for it. There are no storage costs since the newsvendor throws away all unsold products at the end of the day.*

*To maximize profit, use the underage and overage costs to calculate the critical fractile.*

*Critical fractile = underage cost / (underage cost + overage cost)*

*Critical fractile = $2.00 / ($2.00 + $0.50) = 0.80*

*The critical fractile of 0.80 means that you should stock newspapers at the 80th percentile of the demand distribution.*

*In a normal distribution, the 80th percentile corresponds to the point that is 0.842 standard deviations above the mean. This is determined using a normal distribution calculator or table.*

*Since the standard deviation of demand is 20 newspapers, 0.842 standard deviations is roughly 17 newspapers. The mean daily demand is 100 newspapers. So, the optimal inventory level that maximizes profits for the newsvendor is 117 newspapers.*

# Summary

- There are three major types of operations questions

  o Process improvement questions

  o Pricing questions

  o Forecasting and capacity planning questions

- There are four steps to answer process improvement questions:

  o Identify the most important performance metrics

  o Decompose the process into separate, distinct components

  o Use the PPT framework to assess the people, process, and technology for each component

  o Prioritize the most important improvements

- There are three main pricing strategies. Your answer to pricing questions will likely be a mix of these:

  o Pricing based on costs

  o Pricing based on competition

  o Pricing based on value added

- There are three different ways of forecasting

  o Qualitative techniques are used when data is scarce

  o Time series analysis and projection is used when you have several years of stable data

- o Causal models are used when historical data is available and enough analysis has been performed to identify how different factors impact the forecast

- The decision on how much inventory to carry depends on the overage and underage costs.

  - o Carrying too little inventory leads to underage costs, which include the cost of lost sales and the cost of having unsatisfied customers

  - o Carrying too much inventory leads to overage costs, which include storage costs and the loss in profit from discounting unsold inventory

- The optimal inventory level can be calculated using the newsvendor model, which maximizes profit

  - o Determine the underage and overage costs

  - o Calculate the critical fractile

  - o The critical fractile tells you at what percentile on the normal distribution demand curve you should stock inventory to

  - o Based on the percentile, determine how many standard deviations above or below the mean you should stock to

  - o Given the standard deviation of the normal distribution demand curve, calculate the optimal inventory level

# Practice

1. The process of renewing your driver's license typically involves seven steps:

   - Arrive at the local driver license office

   - Complete the renewal application form

   - Provide proper documentation to verify your identity

   - Pass the vision exam

   - Provide thumbprints

   - Have your picture taken

   - Pay the application renewal fee

   How would you improve this process to make it faster?

   *This process has too many steps. There is likely a lot of time wasted in between steps due to waiting and transitioning times.*

   *The amount of time wasted in between steps can be significantly reduced by shifting steps online. The primary advantage of this is that drivers can complete these steps at their own pace without having to wait for a worker to help them.*

   *The renewal application form, submission of proper documentation, submission of a picture, and payment for the application can all be completed online.*

   *It is probably better to administer vision exams and take thumbprints in-person to avoid cheating and fraud.*

   *Making these process changes would require the use of technology. Facial recognition technology is needed to confirm that identification documents match the person that is submitting them. Image processing software is necessary to detect fake documents.*

*Let's look at people next.*

*While workers at driver license offices are capable and trained at doing their jobs, there are opportunities to motivate them better. The bonuses of workers should be tied to the number of people serviced or average waiting times. This would incentivize workers to work more efficiently.*

*In summary, I have two recommendations for improving the driver license renewal process. One, we should shift as many steps of the renewal process online by leveraging technology. Two, we should change the compensation structure of driver license office workers to incentivize quick service.*

2. How should YouTube price its YouTube Premium offering? YouTube Premium removes all ads from videos and gives the user access to exclusive, premium videos.

   *At a minimum, YouTube Premium should be priced to at least recoup its costs.*

   *One cost is the loss of ad revenue from premium users. If the average premium user watches twenty minutes of YouTube a day, that is about two ads per day. This translates to sixty ads per month. If each ad shown generates $0.10 in revenue, YouTube loses $6 per user per month.*

   *Additionally, YouTube also pays YouTubers to produce premium content. Let's assume YouTube pays 1,000 channels about $20,000 per month to create content. This is a monthly cost of $20M. If we believe that one percent of YouTube's 2 billion users purchase premium, that is 20 million users. Therefore, each user would need to pay $1 for YouTube to break even.*

   *From this, YouTube should charge at least $7 per month to recoup its lost ad revenues and costs for producing premium content.*

*However, YouTube can charge higher than this, depending on the value they deliver to customers.*

*Skipping ads saves the customer time. If customers see sixty ads per month and each ad is thirty seconds, that is thirty minutes of time savings. If customers value their free-time at $10 per hour, then skipping ads provides a value of $5 to the customer per month.*

*Additionally, let's say that the average premium user watches fifteen minutes of premium content per week. That is roughly one hour of premium content per month. If customers also value this entertainment at $10 per hour, watching premium content provides a value of $10 to the customer per month.*

*From this, we estimate that YouTube could charge a maximum of $15 per month.*

*In summary, YouTube should charge between $7 - $15 per month for their premium offering. We can look at the price points of competitor offerings, such as Netflix, HBO, and Hulu, to further narrow down the price range.*

3. Amazon is launching its new Kindle device, which is an e-reader that enables users to buy, download, and read digital books, magazines, and other digital media.

   They are planning how much inventory to carry. The Kindle will sell for $80 and costs Amazon $72 to produce. Any inventory shortage leads to a lost sale. Any inventory surplus will be discounted at 25% and sold at the end of the year.

   Amazon estimates the average demand to be one million units with a standard deviation of 300,000 units. If Amazon is looking to maximize profits, how much inventory should they carry?

   *We need to determine the overage and underage costs. If Amazon has excess Kindles, they will be sold at a 25% discount for $60. Since Kindles cost $72 to produce, this is a loss of $12.*

*If Amazon has a shortage of Kindles, Amazon will lose out on the profits of each sale. Amazon makes $8 on each Kindle.*

*Therefore, the critical fractile = $8 / ($8 + $12) = 0.4. Amazon should stock the Kindle at the 40th percentile of the demand distribution, which means it should stock fewer units than the expected average demand of one million units.*

*We can calculate the exact inventory level Amazon should carry. In a normal distribution, the 40th percentile corresponds to the point that is 0.253 standard deviations below the mean. This is determined using a normal distribution calculator or table.*

*Since we know the standard deviation of demand is 300,000 units, 0.253 standard deviations is roughly 75,900 units. Therefore, the right inventory level to maximize profits is 1,000,000 – 75,900 = 924,100 units.*

4. For the company you are interviewing with, select a product. How would you improve the manufacturing or fulfillment process for that product?

5. For the company you are interviewing with, select a new product or service that the company is looking to launch. How would you price that product or service?

6. For the company you are interviewing with, select a product. Is it better to carry too much inventory or too little?

# Mini-Cases for Analytics

## The most common types of questions

Analytics questions focus on assessing your ability to understand, analyze, and interpret data. Analytics interviews may include both technical and non-technical questions.

Non-technical questions do not require specific knowledge of statistics or familiarity with various data computing software packages. You will only need a logical, structured approach.

Technical questions, on the other hand, may ask specific questions on analytics tools such as Tableau, R, SQL, MATLAB, or Python.

If you are interviewing for a technical analytics role, make sure you are familiar with using the data and analytics tools listed in the job description. If you have not used these tools before, you will likely need to learn the basics before the interview.

In this chapter, we will focus on learning how to answer the two most common non-technical analytics questions:

- Estimation questions

- Metrics questions

# Estimation questions

Estimation questions ask you to estimate a particular number or figure by making assumptions and performing calculations.

These questions may seem tough to answer, but with practice, estimation questions become straight forward and repetitive.

For estimation questions, you are not assessed on how close your estimate is to the actual number. You are evaluated on whether you can take a logical, structured approach and whether you are comfortable dealing with numbers.

It is great if your estimate is close to the actual number, but what is more important is demonstrating the way you think about data.

There are two different methods to tackle estimation questions. You can either take a top-down approach or a bottom-up approach.

In a top-down approach, you start with a large number and then refine and break down the number until you get your answer.

In a bottom-up approach, you start with a small number and then build up and increase the number until you get your answer.

Let's illustrate how both of these approaches work by taking a look at an example.

**Example**: How many iPhones does Apple sell in the U.S. each year?

*Using a top-down strategy, you could develop the following approach to answer this question:*

- *Start with the number of people in the U.S.*

- *Estimate the percentage of people that have cell phones*

- *Estimate the percentage of cell phones that are iPhones*

- *Estimate the frequency in which a person purchases a new iPhone each year*

- *Multiply these numbers to determine the number of iPhones sold each year*

*Following this approach, we'll assume a U.S. population size of 320 million people. If 75% of people have cell phones and 30% of cell phones are iPhones, this gives us 72 million iPhones. If a person purchases a new iPhone every two years, that means 36 million iPhones are sold in the U.S. each year.*

*Using a bottom-up strategy, you could develop the following approach:*

- *Start with a single Apple store*

- *Estimate the number of visits per day*

- *Calculate the number of visits per year*

- *Estimate the percentage of visits that lead to purchases*

- *Estimate the percentage of purchases that include the iPhone*

- *Multiply by the number of Apple stores in the U.S. to get the total number of iPhones sold in Apple stores*

- *Estimate the percentage of iPhone sales done through non-Apple stores to determine the number of iPhones sold across all stores*

- *Estimate the percentage of iPhone sales that are done online to determine the total number of iPhones sold in the U.S.*

*Following this approach, let's assume a single Apple store gets 1,000 visits per day. If the store is open 360 days per year, an Apple store gets 360,000 visits per year.*

*If 25% of visits lead to purchases and 60% of purchases include an iPhone, one Apple store sells 54,000 iPhones per year. If there are 300 Apple stores in the U.S., then 16.2 million iPhones are sold in Apple stores each year.*

*If non-Apple stores account for 25% of total iPhone store sales, then 21.6 million iPhones are sold in physical stores each year. If online iPhone sales account for 40% of total iPhone purchases, then 36 million iPhones are sold in the U.S.*

As you can see, both the top-down and bottom-up strategy can lead you to the same answer. When answering estimation questions, choose the approach that is easier for you. Most people find the top-down strategy to be simpler.

# Metrics questions

Metrics questions ask you to determine what metrics you would look at when analyzing the performance of a product, feature, or business decision.

There are three steps to answering metrics questions:

1.  Identify which qualities are most important

2.  Brainstorm potential metrics for each quality

3.  Select metrics that are accurate and feasibly measured

Let's take a look at an example.

**Example**: Quora is a question-and-answer website where questions are asked, answered, and edited by internet users. What metrics can Quora use to identify spam?

*To determine the best metrics, let's first look at the distinguishing characteristics of spam.*

*One characteristic is that spam posts repeat the same messages and wording. A useful metric to detect spam would be to measure the similarity of a new post with each existing post on Quora. If the latest post is almost identical to an existing one, then it is likely spam.*

*A second characteristic is that spammers typically copy and paste messages into Quora's text box instead of typing them directly. One potential metric would be to measure the time it takes for a user to submit a post once they begin typing. However, this could be a poor metric because many legitimate Quora users type their answers in a separate word document before transferring them to Quora.*

*A third characteristic is that spammers post many times in a short period. A helpful metric to detect spam would be to measure how frequently a user has made a post. If the frequency is very high, the user could be a spammer. However, there is a risk of incorrectly detecting spammers because some legitimate Quora users are very productive at answering many questions in a short period.*

*A fourth characteristic is that spam postings typically come from newer accounts. Monitoring account age can help identify spam.*

*In summary, creating a metric that measures the similarity of a new post with each existing post would be the most effective metric to identify spam. Metrics measuring the number of posts per hour for new accounts that are less than three weeks old could also be used to supplement this metric.*

# Summary

- Estimation questions ask you to estimate a number or figure by making assumptions and performing calculations

- For estimation questions, you are evaluated on whether you can take a logical, structured approach and whether you are comfortable dealing with numbers

- There are two methods to tackle estimation questions

    o In a top-down approach, you start with a large number and then refine and break down the number until you get your answer

    o In a bottom-up approach, you start with a small number and then build up and increase the number until you get your answer

- Metrics questions ask you to determine what metrics you would look at when analyzing the performance of a product, feature, or business decision

- There are three steps to answering metrics questions

    o Identify which qualities are most important

    o Brainstorm potential metrics for each quality

    o Select metrics that are accurate and feasibly measured

# Practice

1. How many TV ads are shown in the U.S. each day?

   *One potential approach could look like the following:*

   - *Estimate the number of TV channels in the U.S.*

   - *Assume each channel is on-air for 24 hours each day*

   - *Estimate the percentage of airtime that is given to ads*

   - *Estimate the average duration of an ad*

   - *Divide total ad airtime by ad duration to determine how many TV ads are shown in the U.S.*

   *Starting with the number of TV channels, let's assume there are 2,000 channels. If each channel is on-air for 24 hours each day, that gives us 2,000 * 24 = 48,000 hours of airtime each day.*

   *Let's say that ads take up approximately one-fourth of total airtime. Therefore, ads run for 1/4 * 48,000 = 12,000 hours each day.*

   *The average duration of an ad is estimated to be 30 seconds or 0.5 minutes. 12,000 hours is the equivalent of 720,000 minutes.*

   *So, 720,000 minutes divided by 0.5 minutes per ad gives 1,440,000 TV ads that are shown in the U.S. each day.*

2. What is the market size of electric toothbrushes in the U.S.?

   *Market size is defined as the total dollars of sales of a product or service in one year. One potential approach could be:*

   - *Start with the U.S. population*

   - *Estimate the percentage that brushes their teeth*

- *Estimate the percentage that uses electric toothbrushes*

- *Estimate how many electric toothbrushes the average person purchases each year*

- *Estimate the cost of an electric toothbrush*

- *Multiply all of these figures to determine the market size of electric toothbrushes in the U.S.*

*We'll assume there are roughly 320 million people in the U.S. Assume that 90% of the population brushes their teeth. This leaves us with 320M \* 90% = 288M people.*

*Assume that 25% of people use electric toothbrushes. That gives us 288M \* 25% = 72M people.*

*Let's estimate that a person buys a new electric toothbrush every three years. This means that 72M / 3 = 24M electric toothbrushes are purchased every year.*

*If the average electric toothbrush costs $50, then the market size is 24M \* $50 = $1.2B.*

3. Airbnb is launching a new feature, "5-star listing." This feature would indicate which listings have at least a 4.8 rating. How would you assess the impact of this feature?

    *We can assess how this feature impacts hosts, guests, and Airbnb's bottom line.*

    *For hosts, we hope that this feature would make them happier and stay on the platform. To measure this, we can look at how the net promoter score of hosts has changed since the launch of this feature.*

    *We can also look at how the number of monthly active hosts has changed. An active host can be defined as someone that lists their property in a given month.*

*For guests, this feature should make booking selection easier. We can measure the time it takes for a guest to search through listings and make a booking. We can also measure the booking rate for guests, which is the percentage of site visits that lead to a booking.*

*For Airbnb, we want to see if this feature increases revenues. The number of monthly bookings can measure this. We could also measure the average booking value since five-star listings could be priced higher due to their perceived quality.*

*The goal of this feature is to keep hosts happy and to make bookings easier for guests. Therefore, the two most important metrics to measure are host net promoter score and guest booking rate.*

4. Spotify is a digital music service that gives users access to millions of songs for a monthly or annual subscription fee. Name five key performance indicators for Spotify and what data you would use.

*The most important qualities Spotify should measure are user growth and user engagement. If Spotify has high user growth and high user engagement, then they are likely performing well.*

*One, we can look at monthly active users and how it changes each month. This will give a sense of how many current users Spotify has and whether it is growing or shrinking. Active will be defined as having opened the app at least once in a given month.*

*Two, we can look at the change in the number of new users for each month. The number of new users can be defined as the number of new accounts created. This will give a measure of Spotify's new customer growth rate.*

*Three, for a previous month, we can compare how many active users last month are still active this month. This will give a measure of Spotify's existing user attrition rate.*

*Four, we can look at the number of monthly app opens. This will measure how frequently users engage with Spotify.*

*Five, we can look at the monthly duration of app usage. This will give us a measure of how long users engage with Spotify each time they open the app.*

5.  For the company you are interviewing with, select a product or a feature of the product. What are the most important metrics to monitor?

# Mini-Cases for Finance

## The most common types of questions

Finance questions assess your ability to oversee the profit and loss of the company, manage budgets, and make smart financial decisions.

There are three common types of questions you may get asked:

- Profitability questions

- Budget questions

- Finance and accounting questions

In this chapter, we'll learn effective strategies to answer profitability and budget questions. Then, we'll review the fundamental financial and accounting concepts you should know. Depending on the role you are interviewing for, you may be assessed on your knowledge of these topics.

## Profitability questions

Profitability questions ask how you would assess the profitability of a business or project and identify opportunities for improvement.

There are four steps to answering profitability questions:

1. Break down profit into revenues and costs

2. Break down revenues into its respective components

3. Break down costs into its respective components

4. Identify the best ways to improve profitability

The overall goal of this process is to identify all of the drivers that contribute to profitability. Once you have done this, you can determine which drivers have the largest impact on profitability.

First, break down profit into revenues and costs. Then, further break down revenue into the quantity sold and price.

For price, you can consider whether increasing prices could improve profitability. You can also look at whether switching to a different pricing model could help.

For the quantity sold, you can further break this down by product line, geography, or customer segment. You can compare different segments to see which ones are performing well and which ones are performing poorly.

You can focus on improving the underperforming segments or you can focus on making the high-performing ones do even better.

If improving sales of existing products is not possible, you can also consider adding additional products or services that would help increase profitability.

Afterward, move onto costs to repeat the same process. Break down costs into fixed costs and variable costs.

In general, fixed costs tend to be more difficult to reduce because they have obligations that last for many years. However, fixed costs can be reduced by renegotiating existing contracts or by refinancing contracts for more favorable terms.

Variable costs tend to be easier to reduce. The company can switch to a cheaper supplier, switch to using cheaper substitutes, or use fewer materials in production.

After diving deeper into the components of revenues and costs, this will bring you to the final step.

Among all of the drivers identified, which drivers have the greatest impact on profit? Which drivers have the largest opportunity for improvement? These two questions will help you determine the best ways to improve profitability.

**Example**: How would you improve the profitability of Google Maps?

*To determine how to improve profitability, I will first look at revenues and then costs.*

*On the revenue side, I know that Google Maps primarily makes money by showing advertising when a user performs a search. Revenue is determined by the price that businesses pay Google to show their ads and the number of times ads are shown.*

*To increase profitability, we can look into increasing the price that businesses pay to show their ads. However, the price is determined by an auction-bidding system that depends on the budgets set by companies. This will likely be difficult to change.*

*Therefore, to increase revenues, we can market to businesses to convince more of them to advertise on Google Maps. The increase in demand for advertising on Google Maps could drive higher overall bids.*

*To increase the number of times ads are shown, we need to increase either the number of users of Google Maps or the frequency in which users open up Google Maps. The latter is more difficult to do since it involves changing consumer behavior. Therefore, we should focus on increasing Google Maps' market share among users.*

*We'll look at costs next. There are many different costs of running Google Maps, such as maintenance costs, operating costs, and development costs to add new features.*

*Maintenance and operating costs should not be reduced since they are necessary to keep Google Maps running. However, there may be opportunities to decrease development costs by only focusing on adding relevant features that users care about.*

*In summary, there are three major ways Google Maps can increase profitability. Google can increase the number of businesses that run ads on Google Maps, increase its market share among map users, and decrease development costs.*

# Budget questions

Budget questions ask how you would allocate a finite amount of cash or resources across multiple business units or projects. The key to answering budget questions is to have a structured and data-driven methodology.

Zero-based budgeting is a helpful approach in allocating a budget. In zero-based budgeting, you start with your budget and justify every expense that you make.

There are four steps to using this method:

1.  Start with your full budget and reset all expenses to zero

2.  Identify business-critical functions and allocate budget to meet these expenses first

3.  Prioritize the remaining discretionary spending based on quantitative metrics assessing expected returns

4.  Make adjustments if needed to diversify your investments to hedge risks

The goal of this method is to justify every single expense to ensure that you are focusing on investing in the most valuable business units and projects. This way, you determine the budget based on the value that business units and projects bring rather than on how much budget was previously allocated to them.

First, start with a full budget and reset all obligated expenses to zero.

Second, identify the business-critical expenses. These are expenses that need to be paid or else the company cannot exist or operate.

The remaining budget is your discretionary spending. This type of spend is not necessary to keep the company afloat but helps to improve or grow the company.

Third, make a list of all of the different business units or projects that are asking for funding. You will be quantitatively assessing each of these to determine which investments will be the best use of money.

The most common way of doing this is to forecast future earnings from these business units or projects to determine which provides the highest net present value.

If you are unfamiliar with what net present value is, the next section in this chapter provides an overview of the fundamental finance knowledge you should know.

Ideally, you would allocate money to all projects that have a positive net present value. If you run out of budget, you may want to consider raising debt to finance additional projects. However, the company may not want to take on more debt. In this case, allocate budget to projects with the highest net present value.

Now that you have allocated the entire budget, the fourth step is to check how diversified your investments are and modify the allocations to each business unit or project if needed.

Budget diversification is beneficial because it reduces risk. If one project has the highest net present value but requires your entire budget, you may not want to invest in it because if that project fails, you will get no returns.

Instead, if you had invested in three different projects that all have positive net present values, this would be less risky. It is less likely that you would get no returns because this would require all three projects to fail.

Use your discretion and the company's risk tolerance to determine if the budget allocation is sufficiently diversified.

**Example**: How would you allocate a quarterly budget for Facebook's social media platform?

*I would first allocate budget towards business-critical functions. These are expenses that are necessary to keep Facebook's social media platform up and running. These would be the costs of maintaining and running the website.*

*Other expenses, such as research and development and marketing, are important, but not business-critical expenses.*

*The remaining budget is discretionary spending. I would allocate budget on investments that have the highest net present value for the company.*

*For example, if there are three investments with net present values of $100M, -$200M, and $400M, I'd prioritize allocating budget towards the investment that generates $400M in net present value.*

*If there is remaining budget left, I would also invest in the $100M net present value investment. If there is no budget remaining, I would see if it is possible to take on debt to finance the project since it has a positive net present value.*

*Once all of the discretionary spending is allocated, I would check to see that there is a diversity of different projects and investments being made. It would be very risky to invest all discretionary spending into a single project, even if it has the highest net present value.*

*For example, investing in two different projects that have a net present value of $10M and $20M would be less risky than investing in one project that has a net present value of $30M.*

*At a high-level, this is the process and thinking I would go through to allocate a budget.*

# Finance and accounting questions

In this section, we'll review the essential finance and accounting information you should know.

**Four main financial statements**

**Income statement**: This financial statement illustrates the profitability of the company and covers a specified period, such as a quarter or year.

The income statement starts with revenues and subtracts expenses, such as the following:

- Cost of goods sold

- Selling, general, and administrative expenses

- Other operating expenses

- Depreciation or amortization

- Interest expenses

- Taxes

The result is net income, which is a measure of profitability.

**Balance sheet**: This financial statement shows the company's assets, liabilities, and shareholder's equity. The balance sheet represents a snapshot in time, such as at the end of a quarter or year.

Assets are resources that the company has while liabilities and shareholder's equity are funding sources for those resources. The key equation for the balance sheet is that assets must always equal the sum of liabilities and shareholder's equity.

**Statement of cash flows**: This financial statement shows the inflow and outflow of cash for the company over a specified period, such as a quarter or year.

There are three main uses of cash, which the statement of cash flows breaks out:

- Operating activities: Use of cash related to producing net income, which includes purchasing inventory, paying salaries, and paying for other operating expenses

- Investing activities: Use of cash related to investments in long-term assets, which includes purchasing land, buildings, and equipment

- Financing activities: Use of cash related to raising money from debt or stock, which includes issuing bonds, purchasing treasury stock, and repaying debt

**Statement of shareholder's equity**: This statement shows how shareholder's equity has changed over a specified period, such as a quarter or year. This includes activities such as issuing new shares for cash, purchasing treasury stock, and issuing dividends.

**Cash accounting versus accrual accounting**

There are two fundamentally different types of accounting, cash accounting and accrual accounting.

Cash accounting recognizes revenues and expenses when money changes hands. Accrual accounting recognizes revenue when it is earned, which is when the product or service is delivered, and it recognizes expenses when they are billed, not when they are paid.

In the U.S., the generally accepted accounting principles (GAAP) require accrual accounting because it presents a more accurate picture of a company's financial condition. However, most small businesses use cash accounting because it is simpler.

**Time value of money**

One of the key concepts in finance is that money available today is worth more than an identical amount of money in the future due to its potential earning capacity.

*Example: If you had $100 today, you could invest that money in the stock market to earn an expected return of 6% per year. After one year, you would have $106. Therefore, if someone were to pay you $106 one year from today, that would be the same as someone paying you $100 today.*

To calculate today's value of future cash flows, also known as the present value, use the following formula:

$PV = C / (1 + r)^n$

What each variable means:

- PV = present value

- C = cash flow at a certain period in the future

- r = discount rate, which is also known as the opportunity cost of money

- n = number of periods the cash flow is in the future

**Example**: Would you rather receive $101 today, $108 one year from today, or $114 two years from today? Assume that the opportunity cost of money is investing in the stock market, which generates expected returns of 6% per year.

*To make this decision, we need to calculate the present value of all three of the options. The discount rate, or opportunity cost of money, in this example is 6%.*

*Receiving $101 today has a present value of $101 by definition.*

*Receiving $108 one year from today has a present value less than $108 due to the time value of money. We can calculate its present value:*

*PV = $108 / (1 + 6%) = $101.89*

*Receiving $114 two years from today also has a present value less than $114 due to the time value of money. Its present value is calculated as:*

*PV = $114 / (1 + 6%)² = $101.46*

*Therefore, receiving $108 one year from today is the best option because it has the highest present value. We get the most money from this decision.*

## Evaluating investments

There are two common ways in which companies evaluate investment opportunities: net present value (NPV) and internal rate of return (IRR).

**Net present value**: NPV is used to determine the present value of all future cash flows generated by a project, which includes the initial capital investment.

The higher the NPV, the more desirable a project is to undertake. However, as long as the NPV is greater than zero, the company should pursue the project because it would generate incremental cash or profit for the company.

**Example**: Uber has a user interface improvement project that would cost $10M today. The improvements in their app's interface would create an incremental profit of $2M in its first year, $4M in its second year, and $8M in its third year.

Use a discount rate of 10%, which is the return that Uber can get from using the cash for other purposes. What is the net present value of this project?

*PV of cash flow today = -$10M*

*PV of cash flow in one year = $2M / (1 + 10%) = $1.818M*

*PV of cash flow in two years = $4M / (1 + 10%)$^2$ = $3.306M*

*PV of cash flow in three years = $8M / (1 + 10%)$^3$ = $6.011M*

*Net present value = -$10M + $1.818M + $3.306M + $6.011M = $1.134M*

*The net present value of this project is $1.134M. Since this is greater than zero, the company should pursue this project.*

**Internal rate of return**: The IRR is the discount rate that makes the net present value of all cash flows from a project equal to zero.

The higher the IRR, the more desirable a project is to undertake. However, as long as the IRR is greater than the company's discount rate, the company should pursue the project. This is because the company would be generating more cash than it normally could.

**Example**: Calculate the IRR of Uber's improvement project in the previous example.

*Start with the formula for NPV.*

$$NPV = -\$10M + [\$2M/(1 + R\%)] + [\$4M/(1 + R\%)^2] + [\$8M/(1 + R\%)^3]$$

*Set NPV = 0 and solve for R.*

*R = 15.1%*

*The IRR of the project is 15.1%. Therefore, Uber should pursue the project because the IRR is greater than Uber's discount rate of 10%.*

## Capital structure and cost of capital

Companies run their businesses by using the capital they raise. Companies can raise capital either through equity or debt.

Equity includes selling shares of the company on the stock exchange or to private investors. Debt includes issuing interest-paying bonds or taking loans.

Capital structure is the particular combination of debt and equity used by a company to finance its operations. A company's discount rate comes from its weighted average cost of capital (WACC).

Capital raised through equity and debt have different costs. The WACC is the average after-tax cost of a company's capital sources. This is the discount rate that projects need to exceed for the company to pursue them.

If the WACC is higher than the IRR of a project, it does not make sense for the company to pursue the project. The project's returns are lower than the company's cost of capital to pursue that project.

WACC is calculated using the following formula:

$$WACC = (E \ / \ V * R_e) + [D \ / \ V * R_d * (1 - T_c)]$$

What each variable means:

- $E$ = market value of the company's equity

- $D$ = market value of the company's debt

- $V = E + D$

- $R_e$ = cost of equity

- $R_d$ = cost of debt

- $T_c$ = corporate tax rate

As you can see, the WACC formula is simply a weighted average of the cost of equity and the cost of debt determined by the percentage of capital the company finances with equity versus debt.

One advantage of debt is that interest on debt is a tax-deductible expense. Therefore, taking on debt creates a tax shield, which lowers the cost of capital because the company pays less in taxes.

$R_e$ is the cost of equity and is calculated by using the Capital Asset Pricing Model (CAPM):

$$R_e = R_f + \beta * (R_m - R_f)$$

What each variable means:

- $R_f$ = risk-free rate

- $\beta$ = beta of the investment

- $R_m$ = expected return of the market

The risk-free rate is the theoretical rate of return of an investment with zero risk. This is usually measured by the returns of U.S. treasury bills, in which risks of default are extremely low.

Beta measures the volatility of a security in comparison to the market as a whole. If a stock has a beta greater than one, it is riskier than the market. If a stock has a beta less than one, it will reduce the risk of a market portfolio.

The expected return of the market is typically measured by average annual returns of a stock index, such as the S&P 500, which measures the performance of 500 large companies listed on stock exchanges in the U.S.

**Example**: Given the following information, what is the WACC of this company?

- Risk-free rate, represented by annual return on a 20-year treasury bond, is 2%

- Beta for the company is 0.5

- The average market return, represented by the average annualized returns for the S&P 500 index, is 10%

- Shareholder's equity is $80B, taken from the balance sheet

- Long term debt stands at $40B, taken from the balance sheet

- The cost of debt is 6%

- Corporate tax rate is 30%

*To solve this, we'll use the WACC formula.*

$V = E + D = \$80B + \$40B = \$120B$

$R_e = R_f + \beta * (R_m - R_f) = 2\% + 0.5 * (10\% - 2\%) = 6\%$

$WACC = (E / V * R_e) + [D / V * R_d * (1 - T_c)]$

$WACC = (\$80B / \$120B * 6\%) + [\$40B / \$120B * 6\% * (1 - 30\%)]$

$WACC = 5.4\%$

*The weighted average cost of capital for the company is 5.4%.*

### Determining the valuation of companies

While there are many ways to value a company, you should be familiar with the following six methods:

**Market capitalization**: This method determines a company's valuation by multiplying the company's share price by the total number of shares outstanding.

**Discounted Cash Flow (DCF)**: First, forecast all future cash flows of the company. Then, discount all cash flows to the present day using the company's discount rate. The resulting net present value is the company's valuation.

**Comparable companies' multiples**: This method uses the metrics of other similarly sized businesses in the same industry to determine a valuation. The two most common metrics used are the P/E ratio and the EV/EBITDA multiple.

The P/E ratio stands for price to earnings. It measures a company's current share price relative to its earnings per share.

The EV/EBITDA ratio stands for enterprise value to earnings before interest, taxes, depreciation, and amortization. It measures the company's total value relative to a measure of the company's cash earnings in one year.

If you know the P/E or EV/EBITDA ratio of other similar companies, you can use these ratios to determine the valuation.

**Cost approach**: This method values the company by estimating the cost it would take to build the company from nothing.

**Book value**: This method values the company by the value of shareholder's equity on the balance sheet. This can be calculated by subtracting total liabilities from total assets.

**Liquidation value**: This method values a company by determining the cash that the company would receive if it liquidated all of its assets and paid off all of its liabilities.

# Summary

- There are three common types of questions asked in interviews for finance roles

  o Profitability questions

  o Budget questions

  o Finance and accounting questions

- Profitability questions ask how you would assess the profitability of a business or project. There are four steps to answering these questions:

  o Break down profit into revenues and costs

  o Break down revenues into its respective components

  o Break down costs into its respective components

  o Identify the best ways to improve profitability

- Budget questions ask how you would allocate a finite amount of cash or resources across multiple business units or projects. There are four steps to answering these questions:

  o Start with your budget and reset all expenses to zero

  o Identify business-critical functions and allocate budget to meet these expenses first

  o Prioritize the remaining discretionary spending based on quantitative metrics assessing expected returns

  o Make adjustments to diversify your investments or to hedge risks

- You may be asked questions that assess your knowledge of finance and accounting on concepts such as the following:

o   The four main financial statements

o   Cash accounting versus accrual accounting

o   The time value of money

o   Evaluating investments using NPV and IRR

o   Capital structure and cost of capital (WACC)

o   The different ways to value a company

# Practice

1. Select a product or service from the company that you are interviewing with. How would you improve profitability?

2. How would you allocate a limited budget across different business units in a company?

3. What are the four main financial statements? What information does each provide?

   *The four main financial statements are the income statement, balance sheet, statement of cash flows, and statement of shareholder's equity.*

   *The income statement illustrates the profitability of the company over a specified period.*

   *The balance sheet shows the company's assets, liabilities, and shareholder's equity at a point in time.*

   *The statement of cash flow shows how the company has used cash over a specified period.*

   *The statement of shareholder's equity shows how shareholder's equity has changed over a specified period.*

4. How would you evaluate whether to invest in a project?

   *You can evaluate an investment by using net present value (NPV) or internal rate of return (IRR).*

   *Using NPV, investments should only be made if the NPV is greater than zero. Using IRR, investments should only be made if the IRR is greater than the discount rate of the company, which is usually the weighted average cost of capital (WACC).*

5. What is a weighted average cost of capital (WACC)? What is it used for?

*The WACC is a calculation of a company's cost of capital, and is a weighted average of the cost of equity and cost of debt based on the percentage of the company's capital that is financed through each. The WACC provides a discount rate for a company to use when making investment decisions.*

6. What does beta represent in the Capital Asset Pricing Model (CAPM)?

*Beta is a measure of the volatility of a stock in comparison to the market as a whole. Knowing the beta of a stock helps you understand whether the stock moves in the same direction as the market. It also tells you whether the stock is riskier or less risky than the market.*

7. What are the different ways to value a company?

*There are six different ways to value a company.*

*Market capitalization: valuation is determined by multiplying the company's share price by the total number of shares outstanding*

*Discounted cash flow: valuation is determined by calculating the net present value of all future free cash flows of the company*

*Comparable companies' multiples: valuation is determined by using financial ratios of other similarly sized businesses in the same industry*

*Cost approach: valuation is determined by estimating the cost it would take to build the company from nothing*

*Book value: valuation is determined by the value of shareholder's equity on the balance sheet*

*Liquidation value: valuation is determined by estimating the cash the business would get if it sold all assets and paid off all liabilities*

# Data Challenges

# Data Challenge Strategy

## What is a data challenge?

A data challenge is a take-home assignment in which the interviewer will give you a small dataset and a business question to answer. You will analyze and interpret the data and then make presentation slides to communicate your answer.

You will have a limited amount of time to complete the data challenge. Once the interviewer sends you the dataset, you will have anywhere between one to seven days to complete it.

The dataset is usually sent in a Microsoft Excel format. Unless your dataset has millions of rows, you should be able to complete all of your analysis in Excel. However, if you are interviewing for more technical analytics or data science roles, you may need to use other tools, such as Tableau, R, or Python.

After completing the analysis, expect to make between 6 – 12 slides to communicate your findings. Unless specified, you can use any presentation slide-making software or tool. The most common ones include Microsoft PowerPoint, Google Slides, and Apple Keynote.

Once you complete the data challenge, you will submit your presentation slides to the interviewer. In the next interview round, you may be asked to give a presentation of your data challenge findings. There, your interviewer could ask you specific follow-up questions on your work.

## What are interviewers looking for?

Interviewers give data challenges to determine if candidates can do the analytics and slide making that the role requires. There are three main qualities interviewers are looking for:

- Correct execution of data analysis

- Generation of appropriate insights

- Clear and concise presentation slides

For the first bullet point, interviewers want to see that all of your metrics and numbers are calculated correctly. They want to see that you have the attention to detail to double-check your numbers and ensure accuracy.

For the second bullet point, interviewers want to see that you can drive the right insights using the data. You should be able to identify the key takeaways from the data and interpret how they should shape your answer.

For the third bullet point, interviewers want to see that you can communicate your answer or recommendation effectively. Your presentation slides should be easy to follow and succinctly cover all of your main points.

## What is the best way to complete data challenges?

There are seven steps to completing a data challenge:

1. Understanding the objective

2.  Becoming familiar with the data

3.  Cleaning the data

4.  Structuring a framework

5.  Analyzing the data

6.  Synthesizing the data

7.  Making presentation slides

We'll go through each step to learn the most effective strategies to complete the data challenge and make your submission stand out.

## Understanding the objective

The first step in completing a data challenge is to understand what the objective is. What is the primary question you are trying to answer with the data? Answering the wrong question is the quickest way to fail a data challenge.

You will frequently refer back to the primary question when you are analyzing the data. If your analysis does not bring you closer to answering the question, then your analysis is probably unimportant or irrelevant.

You will also refer back to the primary question when you are making presentation slides. If a slide you created doesn't help communicate the answer, then that slide is likely not needed.

Taking the time to fully understand the objective of the data challenge can save you hours of doing unnecessary work.

## Becoming familiar with the data

After understanding the objective of the data challenge, you should familiarize yourself with the dataset. What do the rows represent? What does each column show? This will help you understand what types of analyses are possible.

Typically, each row in a dataset represents an individual response. The columns usually show different metrics or observations.

## Cleaning the data

After becoming familiar with the dataset, check the data quality:

- Are there any duplicated entries?

- Are any entries in the wrong format or structure?

- Is your dataset missing any fields or values?

You may need to do some data cleaning to remove duplicates or to ensure that all data entries are in a consistent, standard format.

If the dataset has missing fields or values, there are three different ways to handle this:

- Remove the row or column entirely

- Estimate the missing values based on other data points

- Leave the dataset as it is

Each of these actions has its own advantages and disadvantages.

Removing the entire row or column is easy to do, but may significantly decrease your sample size. There could be potential cuts of the data that you can no longer analyze because you have fewer data points.

Estimating the missing values based on other data points can be difficult to do, but it keeps the number of data points that can be analyzed as large as possible.

Leaving the dataset untouched is easy to do, but it may skew the results of some of your analyses. Use your judgment on what action makes the most sense.

## Structuring a framework

Before beginning your data analysis, you should create a basic framework to help guide your analysis. You can use the same framework strategy as the one you used for case interviews. Review the "Case Interview Strategy" chapter for a refresher if needed.

Select 3 – 4 broad areas that you think are the most important to analyze. In other words, what are the 3 – 4 things you need to know to answer the primary question of the data challenge?

Your framework will help keep you on track when you begin analyzing the data. It ensures that all of the analyses that you do are relevant and important.

## Analyzing the data

Once you have your framework, you can finally start your analysis. There are three different types of analyses that you will likely do:

- Analyzing basic metrics

- Analyzing compound metrics

- Modeling

The first type of analysis is the simplest. You'll look at all of the different metrics or observations in the dataset to see how they vary across different groups. Make a note of any variations that you see.

*Example*: *You have a dataset of Apple retail stores. Each row in the dataset represents a different retail store. The columns have metrics such as location, annual revenue, annual number of customers, and store square footage. The objective of the data challenge is to determine which retail stores Apple should focus on improving.*

*A basic metric you could analyze is how annual revenue differs across all of the stores. You could propose that Apple focus on improving stores that have the lowest annual revenue.*

The second type of analysis involves creating compound metrics, which are metrics derived from two or more metrics.

Often, you'll find it useful to create a new metric to assess a particular characteristic or quality. To do this, you will need to create a new column or row in Excel and compute the metric.

*Example: For the Apple retail store data challenge, you may want to create a compound metric of revenue per square foot by taking annual revenue and dividing it by store square footage.*

*Annual revenue is a slightly biased metric because larger stores typically have more sales. Therefore, by normalizing annual revenue by square footage, you can see how efficient each store is.*

The third type of analysis is modeling. For some data challenges, you might find it helpful to create some kind of model to make a prediction or forecast based on assumptions and existing data.

*Example: Let's say that you identify that Apple should focus on improving three particular retail stores in Canada. You can use the data on the other stores in Canada and make assumptions on how much improvement is possible. You could then create a model to predict how much annual revenues will increase.*

## Synthesizing the data

When you have completed your analysis, you will need to decide on an answer or recommendation.

Throughout your analysis, you should have been writing down the key takeaways of each metric that you looked at. Look through your key takeaways and decide on what answer they collectively support.

You should not expect every analysis to support your answer. Often, you'll have key takeaways that support your answer, but also key takeaways that go against your answer. You will need to mediate conflicting insights and decide on what is most important.

Regardless of which answer or recommendation you decide on, you should address the opposing insights. This will demonstrate the thoroughness of your analysis and will make your recommendation more credible.

**Making presentation slides**

The goal of making presentation slides is to make your work and recommendation shine. You can do amazing data analysis, but the interviewer won't be able to see this if you can't make great slides.

Your slides need to tell a compelling story that is clear, easy to follow, and well supported by evidence. Use the following structure when making your presentation slides:

- Title

- Executive summary

- Supporting analysis slides

- Risks & mitigations

- Next steps

- Appendix

We'll go through each section to specify what you should include.

**Title**: Your title slide should be simple. Include a title for your presentation and your name. If you'd like, you can also include a logo of the company you are interviewing with.

**Executive summary**: This slide consists entirely of bullet points that summarize your answer and the supporting evidence.

If a person were just to read the executive summary, they should be able to understand the main points of the entire presentation.

Executive summaries tend to be too long and wordy. Therefore, make every effort to make your bullets as concise as possible. Only include the most important key takeaways.

**Supporting analysis slides**: These slides will be the bulk of your presentation. In this section, you will include charts, graphs, tables, or bullet points that support your answer or recommendation.

**Risks & mitigations**: Include a slide that lists the major risks of your recommendation. This demonstrates to the interviewer that you have thoroughly thought through all of the potential implications.

After each risk, list what actions could be taken to mitigate these risks. If you provide a reasonable plan for managing the potential risks, your answer or recommendation will be much stronger.

If the data challenge has a low slide limit, you can leave out this section and put it in the appendix instead.

**Next steps**: Include a few bullet points outlining potential next steps you would take if you had more data or more time. This demonstrates initiative and ownership.

Ask yourself the following questions:

- What other open questions do you have?

- What else would you need to know to feel more confident in your answer or recommendation?

- What could you do to find answers to these questions?

**Appendix**: You can include backup slides in the appendix, which typically does not count towards the slide limit. These are slides that were not important enough to make it into the main presentation.

Backup slides can also be slides that show assumptions or backup calculations to your main supporting analysis slides. Including these slides shows your work to the interviewer and demonstrates attention to detail.

# Additional slide making tips

There are five slide making tips that you should follow to make your presentation stand out.

**Tip #1: Write descriptive slide titles that clearly communicate the main message**

Do not use generic slide titles such as: "Analysis," "Conclusion," or "Findings." These titles do nothing to help the interviewer understand what the main point of the slide is.

Instead, your slide title should clearly communicate the key message of the slide. If the interviewer only reads the title of a slide, they should know what content the slide is going to show.

Additionally, the titles of your slides should collectively read like a story. If the interviewer only read the titles of each slide, they should know everything about your presentation.

**Tip #2: Have one message for each slide**

Avoid having too many tables, graphs, or charts on one slide. This makes the slide dense and difficult to digest. You'll also likely confuse the interviewer by having too many different messages.

The most effective slides have one key message.

If you have too much content on one slide, you either have redundant information or too many messages. If you have redundant information, delete everything that does not add significant incremental value. If you have too many messages, separate the slide into multiple slides.

Conversely, if your slide is barren with minimal content, you either have an undeveloped point or a point that is not important. If the point is undeveloped, combine it with another slide that has the same central message. If the point is not that important, remove it from the presentation.

**Tip #3: Use a variety of different slide formats**

Try to avoid using the same slide format for every slide. This will make your presentation seem dull and repetitive.

Instead, try to use a mixture of different slide formats to keep things interesting. Below are four essential slide formats:

1. Single chart, graph, or table

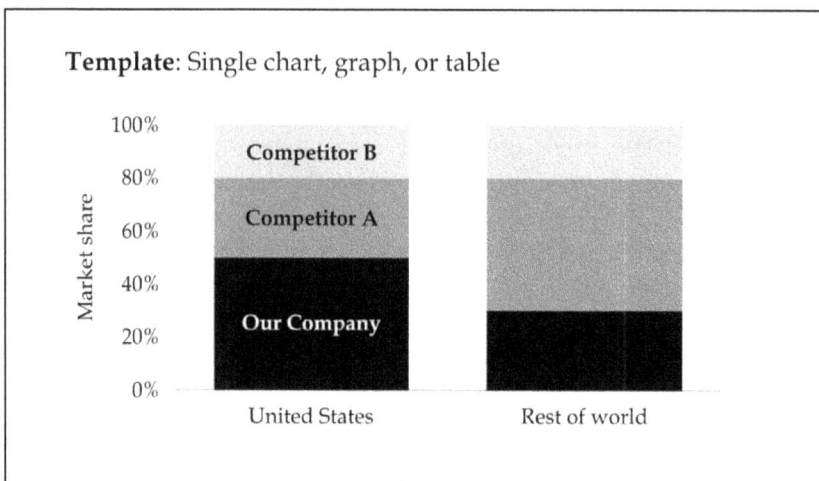

2. Chart, graph, or table with qualitative discussion

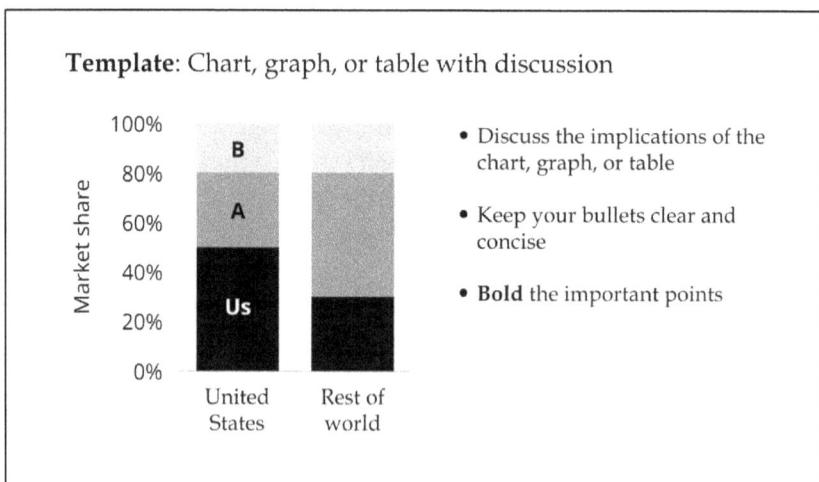

3. Framing slide

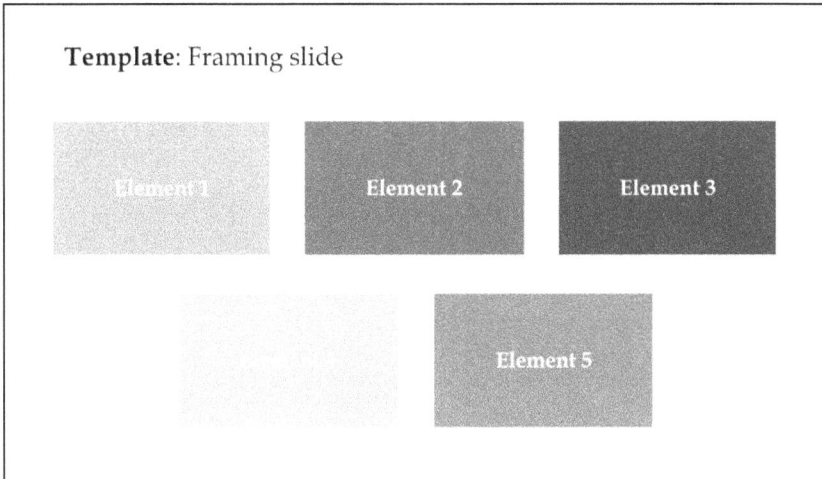

**Template**: Framing slide

| | | |
|---|---|---|
| Element 1 | Element 2 | Element 3 |
| | Element 5 | |

4. Qualitative bullets

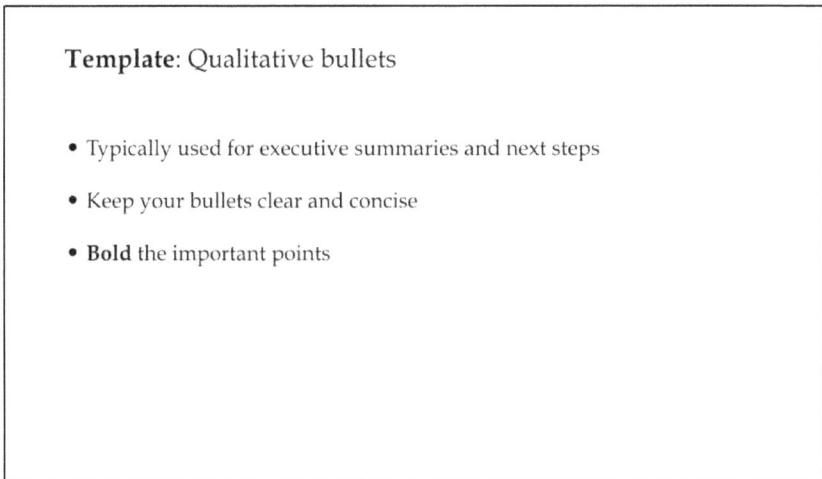

**Template**: Qualitative bullets

- Typically used for executive summaries and next steps
- Keep your bullets clear and concise
- **Bold** the important points

**Tip #4: Call attention to the most important things on each slide**

To make each slide easier to read and digest, you should call attention to the most important things.

After the interviewer reads your slide title, you want to draw their attention to the main takeaway in the slide body.

There are four different ways you can do this:

1. Bold the main points

Selective bolding draws attention and emphasizes points

- Use **selective bolding** to **draw attention** to the most important things

- Bold important numbers, such as **25%** or **$100M**

- Bold **important messages**

- **Do not overuse bolding** or it will lose its effect

2. Circle or box what is important

Circles and boxes draw attention to a particular area

| Year | % of revenue | Price | Cost |
|---|---|---|---|
| **Year 1** | 22% | $4,000 | $1,100 |
| **Year 2** | 23% | $4,000 | $1,200 |
| **Year 3** | 21% | $4,000 | $1,500 |

3. Use a different color to draw attention

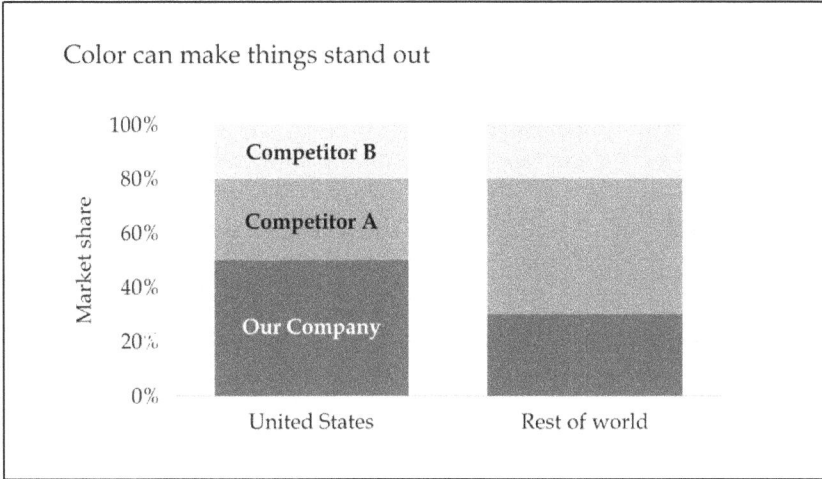

4. Use a callout box

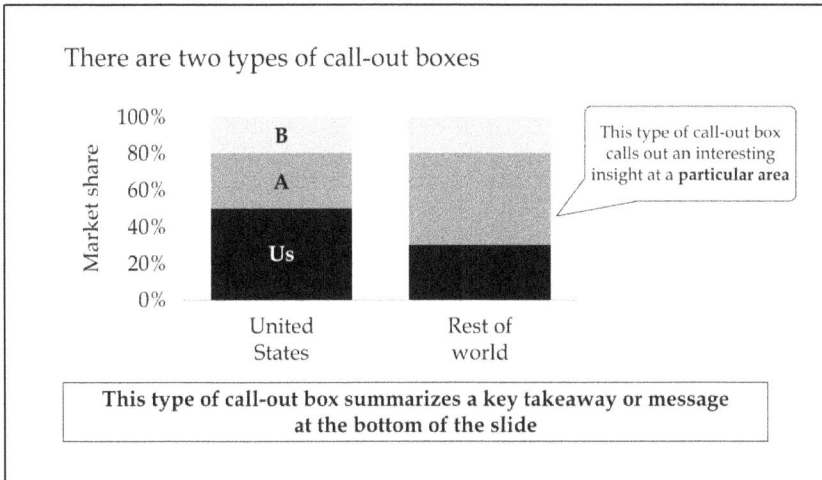

**Tip #5: Use a slide tracker**

To make your presentation easier to follow, you can provide the interviewer with a road map of the presentation before they dive deeper into the supporting analysis slides.

A slide tracker is a visual mechanism, typically located at the top right corner of the slide, that shows the interviewer exactly where they are on the presentation road map.

If you decide that you want to use a slide tracker, make sure that you have a slide laying out the road map of the presentation. Using a slide tracker is not as effective if there is no road map.

Here is an example of how you can use a slide tracker:

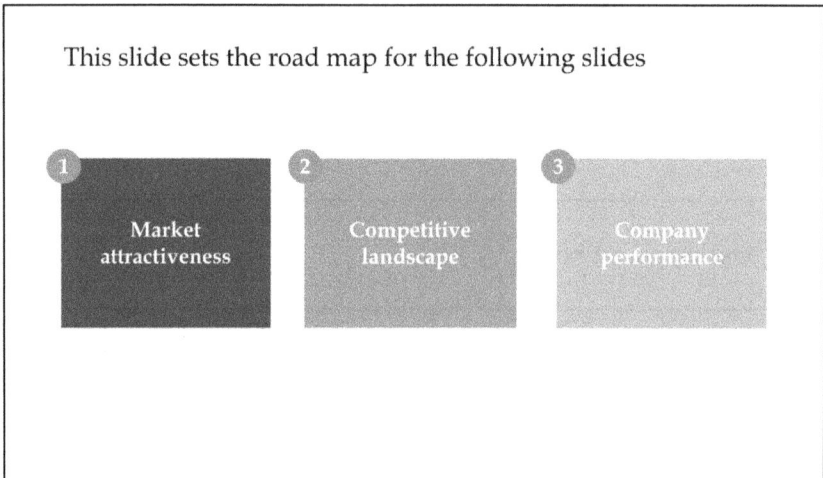

---

2 Competitive landscape

Slide trackers make things easy to follow

- This slide discusses the second area, **competitive landscape**
- The slide tracker on the **top right** indicates this
- The tracker uses the **same color** as what is on the road map slide

---

3 Company performance

Slide trackers make things easy to follow

- This slide discusses the third and last area, **company performance**
- The slide tracker on the **top right** indicates this
- The tracker uses the **same color** as what is on the road map slide

---

# Example of a data challenge

Let's walk through an example of a data challenge.

**Example**: Airbnb is an online marketplace where hosts can offer lodging and homestays for travelers. They are looking to grow the number of hosts on their platform in one of three cities.

Based on the "Listings Dataset," which city should Airbnb prioritize? Keep your presentation to a maximum of eight slides.

You can access the "Listings Dataset" by emailing **conquer.interviews@gmail.com** with the subject "**Get More**". An automated email will send you all supplementary information that comes with this book.

The dataset has three different cities:

- Alpha

- Beta

- Gamma

The dataset contains the following information:

- **Unique Listing ID**: when a host lists a property for rent on Airbnb's platform, it is called a listing. Each row in this dataset represents a different listing and each listing has a unique identification number

- **City**: the city that the property is in

- **# of Nights Listed**: the number of nights in the past year that the listing was published on Airbnb's website. This includes both nights in which the property was booked and nights in which the property was not booked

- **# of Bookings**: the number of times a guest booked a reservation for that listing in the past year. A booking can be for one night or multiple, consecutive nights

- **# of Nights Booked**: the number of nights the property was rented out for in the past year

- **Revenue**: total revenue in U.S. dollars that the listing generated for Airbnb over the past year

*To complete this data challenge, let's go through the seven steps.*

*The first step is to understand the objective. For this data challenge, the goal is to determine which city Airbnb should prioritize growing the number of hosts. We'll need to perform analysis to determine which city is the most attractive.*

*The second step is to become familiar with the data. In this dataset, each row represents a different listing. The first two columns provide the listing identification number and the city that the listing is in. The other four columns provide metrics that were measured over the past year.*

*The third step is to clean the data. In this dataset, there are no duplicated entries, entries in the wrong format or structure, or missing fields or values. We have verified that the dataset is clean and ready to be analyzed.*

*The fourth step is to structure a framework to guide our analysis. Given the data that we have, what qualities would make a city attractive to grow the number of hosts?*

*A few qualities include the following:*

- *The city's listings contribute to a large percentage of revenues*

- *Listings in the city are listed at high prices each night*

- *There is a lot of guest demand for booking stays in the city*

- *Guests book stays in the city for a long period*

- *Many properties in the city are not on Airbnb's platform but could be added to it*

*The fifth step is analyzing the data. Looking at our framework, what metrics would be most useful to analyze?*

*For the first bullet in our framework, we can look at the total revenue generated in each city. This will give us a sense of which city is contributing the most towards Airbnb's total revenues.*

*For the second bullet, we can look at the average revenue per night booked in each city. This is a compound metric calculated by taking revenue and dividing it by the number of nights booked.*

*For the third bullet, we can use listing utilization as a proxy for guest demand. If a property is highly utilized, then that implies there is a high demand for that listing. We can measure utilization by taking the number of nights booked and dividing it by the number of nights listed.*

*For the fourth bullet, we can look at the average number of nights booked per booking, which measures how long guests stay in the property each trip. This is calculated by taking the number of nights booked and dividing it by the number of bookings.*

*For the final bullet, we don't have a metric to directly measure Airbnb's market share among hosts in the city. The best we can do is look at the number of listings in each city.*

*If each city is about the same size, then a smaller number of listings implies that there is more potential to add other properties onto the platform. However, this is probably too big of an assumption to make.*

*The sixth step is to synthesize the data. Once we have finished analyzing all of the metrics of interest, we have the following key takeaways:*

- *Gamma contributed $38,782,140 last year in revenue, the most out of any city*

- *Gamma's average revenue per night booked is $186, the highest out of any city*

- *Gamma's listings have an average utilization of 46%, the highest out of any city*

- *Gamma has an average number of nights booked per booking of 2.2, the highest out of any city*

- *Gamma has the fewest number of listings at 1,802, which may imply that Gamma has the most room for host growth. However, this assumes each city is the same size, which we do not know*

*From these key takeaways, we recommend that Airbnb prioritize growing hosts in Gamma.*

*Moving onto the seventh step, we will need to make presentation slides to communicate our analysis and recommendation.*

*The slides for this data challenge could look like the following:*

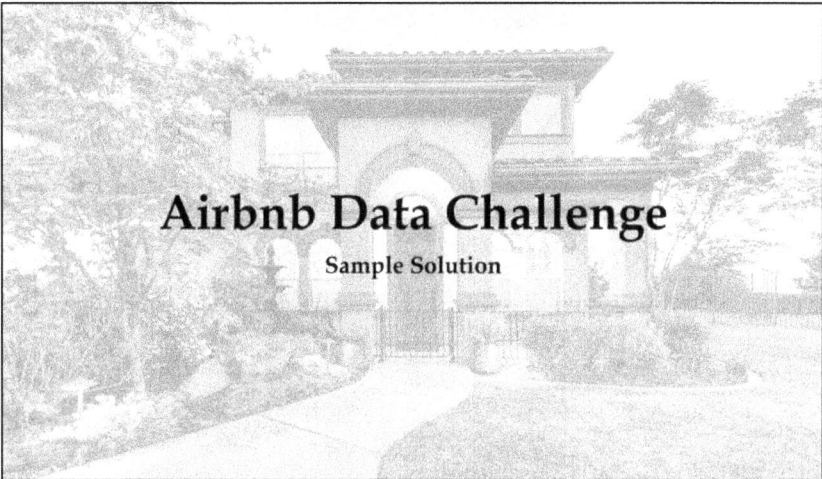

## Executive Summary

- Listings in Gamma make up ~**28%** of all listings, but account for ~**43%** of all revenues

- Listings in Gamma generate the **highest revenue per night booked** ($186) and the **highest average nights booked per booking** (2.2)

- Gamma's listings have the highest average utilization of all cities (**46%**), which may impede guest bookings due to insufficient listing selection

- **Airbnb should focus on growing listings in Gamma**, but needs to verify that there is unmet customer demand, adequate supply of properties to be added, and that there is meaningful future city growth

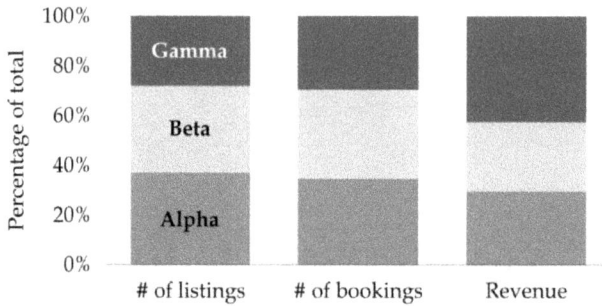

Gamma's listings make up ~28% of total listings, but account for ~30% of bookings and 43% of revenues

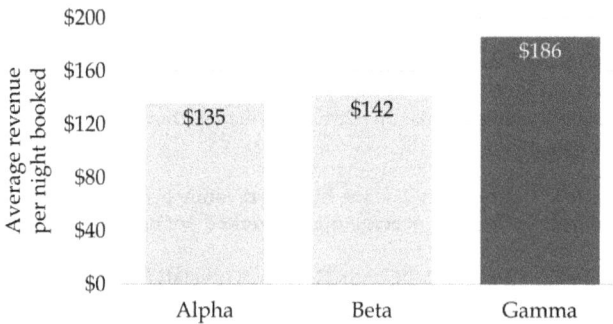

Gamma's listings are lucrative because they generate the highest revenue per night booked at $186 per night

Additionally, Gamma's listings have the highest average nights booked per booking

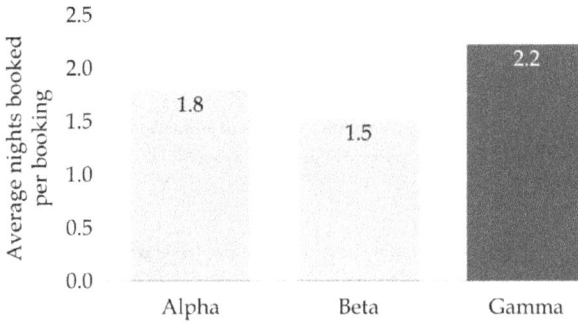

Gamma's listings have the highest average utilization of 46%, which demonstrates high guest demand for listings

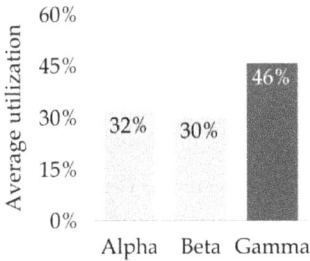

- As utilization increases, guests have **fewer listings to choose from**

- Guests will not make bookings if they **don't find a suitable listing**

- If the number of listings increases, utilization decreases and the **likelihood of customers making a booking increases**

**Airbnb should focus on increasing the number of listings in Gamma**

There are three other factors that Airbnb should consider when prioritizing a city to focus on

**Airbnb's share of guests**
- Determine what **percentage of guests** use Airbnb for each city
- If Airbnb already has a high market share among guests in Gamma, then **there may not be much room for growth**

**Airbnb's share of properties**
- Determine the **percentage of properties** that use Airbnb in each city
- If Airbnb already has a high market share of properties in Gamma, then **there may not be much room for growth**

**Future city growth**
- Determine which cities are the **fastest growing travel destinations**
- Alpha and Beta may be less attractive now, but they **could be very attractive in the future**

---

Next steps

1  Verify that there is **unmet guest demand in Gamma** due to a limited selection of listings during periods of high utilization

2  Confirm that there is a **meaningful number of properties in Gamma** that Airbnb could **add to its platform**

2  Estimate the impact of growing the number of listings in Gamma on **Airbnb's revenues**

# Summary

- A data challenge is a take-home assignment in which the interviewer will give you a small dataset and a business question to answer

- There are seven steps to completing a data challenge

    o Understanding the objective

    o Becoming familiar with the data

    o Cleaning the data

    o Structuring a framework

    o Analyzing the data

    o Synthesizing the data

    o Making presentation slides

- There are three types of analyses you will likely do:

    o Analyzing basic metrics

    o Analyzing compound metrics

    o Modeling

- Use the following structure when making your slides:

    o Title

    o Executive summary

    o Supporting analysis slides

    o Risks & mitigations

- o   Next steps

- o   Appendix

- Follow these five slide making tips to make your presentation stand out from other candidates

  - o   Write descriptive slide titles that clearly communicate the main message

  - o   Have one message for each slide

  - o   Use a variety of different slide formats

  - o   Call attention to the most important things

  - o   Use a slide tracker

# Data Challenge Practice

## Data Challenge #1: Uber Driver Prioritization

Uber is looking to improve driver satisfaction and retention, but they don't have the resources or capacity to focus on all drivers.

Based on the "Driver Dataset," which driver segment should Uber focus on? Keep your presentation to a maximum of ten slides.

You can access the "Driver Dataset" by emailing **conquer.interviews@gmail.com** with the subject "**Get More**". An automated email will send you all supplementary information that comes with this book.

Uber has four segments of drivers:

- **Urban FT**: Full-time drivers that drive in urban areas

- **Urban PT**: Part-time drivers that drive in urban areas

- **Suburban**: Drivers that drive in suburban areas

- **Rural**: Drivers that drive in rural areas

The dataset contains the following information:

- **Unique ID**: a unique identification number for each driver. In the dataset, each row represents a different driver

- **Driver Segment**: the segment that the driver belongs to

- **Revenue**: total revenue generated for Uber over the past year in terms of U.S. dollars

- **# of Trips**: number of trips completed over the past year

- **Driver Satisfaction**: self-reported driver satisfaction on a 1 – 5 scale. "1" is low satisfaction and "5" is high satisfaction

- **Average Rider Satisfaction**: an average of the driver's ratings on a 1 – 5 scale given by all riders over the past year. "1" is low satisfaction and "5" is high satisfaction

- **Drives for Competitor**: self-reported indication of whether the driver also drives for a competitor; "1" indicates that the driver also works for a competitor while "0" indicates that the driver only works for Uber

*One potential solution could look like the following:*

**Uber Data Challenge**
Sample Solution

## Executive Summary

- Urban FT drivers are an important segment that make up **~48% of revenue** even though they only account for ~21% of drivers

- These drivers have the **highest revenue per trip ($17.75)** and have the **highest average rider satisfaction score (4.84 / 5)**

- However, Uber may lose these drivers since they have the **lowest driver satisfaction score (3.1 / 5) and ~41% of them also drive for a competitor**

- Uber should launch a **driver loyalty program for Urban FT drivers**, focusing on providing **bonuses**, **priority customer service**, and **opportunities for drivers to give Uber feedback**

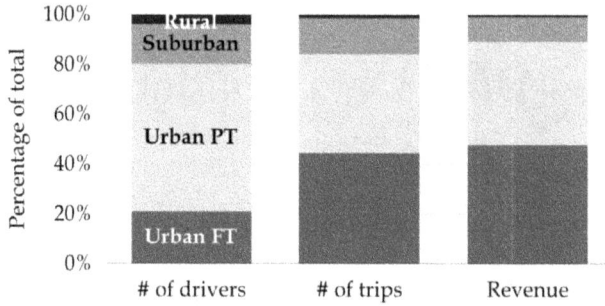

Urban FT drivers make up ~21% of drivers, but account for ~48% of revenue

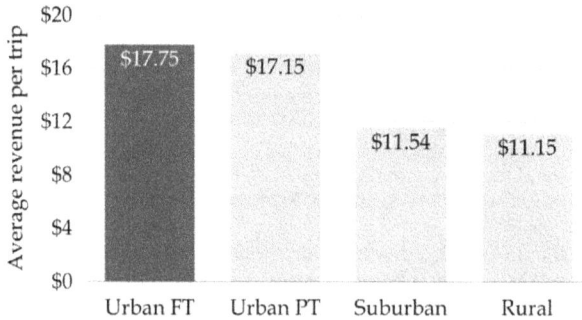

Urban FT drivers make the highest revenue per trip

## Urban FT drivers have the highest rider satisfaction scores

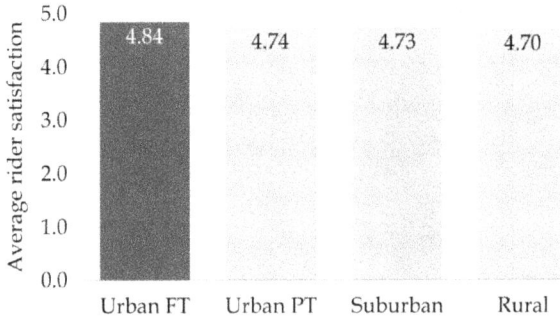

## However, urban FT drivers have the lowest driver satisfaction scores, which may contribute to driver attrition

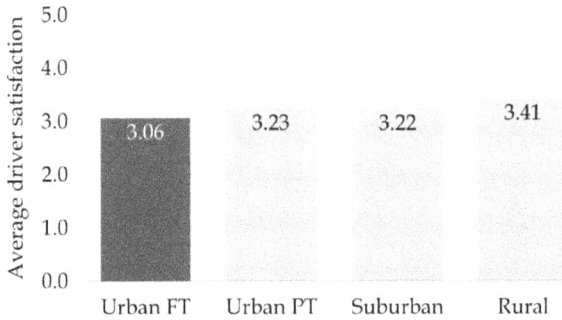

Additionally, ~41% of urban FT drivers also drive for a
competitor, which is much higher percentage than other segments

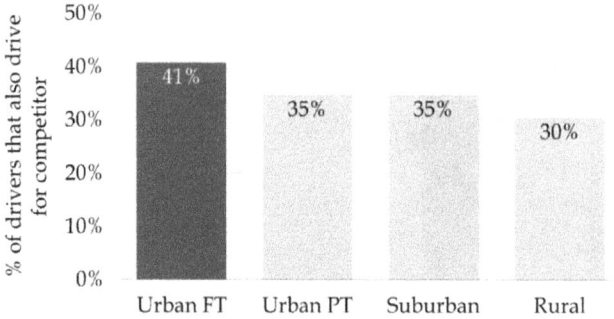

Uber should focus on making urban FT drivers happier
through a driver loyalty program focused on three things

| Bonuses | Priority customer service | Opportunity to give Uber feedback |
|---|---|---|
| • Provide cash bonuses to incentivize drivers to drive more | • Decrease waiting times for driver support | • Ask for suggestions on how to make Uber better for drivers |
| • Celebrate driving anniversaries or driving milestones | • Give an exclusive number to dial or a personal support agent | • Continuously look for improvement opportunities |

## There are three major risks that Uber should consider

**Alienation of other driver segments**

- An urban FT loyalty program may send the unintended message that **Uber only cares about their urban FT drivers**
- Other driver segments may be upset and **leave Uber's platform**

**Driver pay war**

- Uber's competitors may also **increase bonuses** for drivers
- This could create a **driver pay war** to win driver loyalty, which would be costly for all ride-sharing app companies

**Impact on Uber's profitability**

- Uber needs to determine the **costs of the driver loyalty program**
- They need to understand if the costs **justify the increase in retention of urban FT drivers**

## Next steps

1. Understand why urban FT drivers have **low satisfaction**
2. Benchmark against **what competitors are doing to retain their drivers**
3. Assess the **financial impact** of launching a **driver loyalty program**

# Data Challenge #2: Google Ads Growth

Businesses pay Google to display search-based advertising on Google's search engine. One of Google's goals this year is to grow its ads business. They can do this by either targeting new customers or increasing revenues among existing customers.

Based on the "Ads Dataset," what are the five most important insights or recommendations that you have? Keep your presentation to strictly five slides that show your analysis.

You can access the "Ads Dataset" by emailing **conquer.interviews@gmail.com** with the subject "**Get More**". An automated email will send you all supplementary information that comes with this book.

The dataset contains the following information:

- **Customer ID**: Each row in the dataset represents a different customer that buys advertising from Google. Each customer has a unique identification number

- **Customer Type**: Customers are categorized as either new customers or existing customers. New customers are those that started advertising with Google less than one year ago. Existing customers are those that started advertising with Google more than one year ago

- **Customer Industry**: This indicates the industry that the customer's business is in. There are five industries: Consumer, Finance, Health, Technology, and Travel

- **Payment Structure**: Customers have the option to pay for their advertising through one of two ways:

  - **CPC** stands for cost per click. The customer pays a certain amount each time someone clicks their ad

  - **CPM** stands for cost per thousand impressions. The customer pays a certain amount for every one thousand impressions. An impression occurs when the ad is displayed and viewed by someone

- **Revenue**: This is the amount that the customer paid Google for advertising over the past year

- **Impressions**: This is the number of times the customer's ads were displayed and viewed over the past year.

- **Clicks**: This is the number of times the customer's ads were clicked over the past year

- **Customer Satisfaction**: Customers can give feedback in their Google ads account on their satisfaction level with the service they are receiving. A "1" indicates that the customer is happy with Google ads. A "0" indicates that the customer is unhappy with Google ads

*One potential solution could look like the following:*

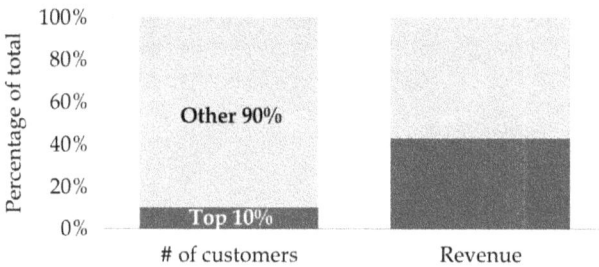

Finance customers have an average annual revenue of $148K, the highest of any customer industry segment

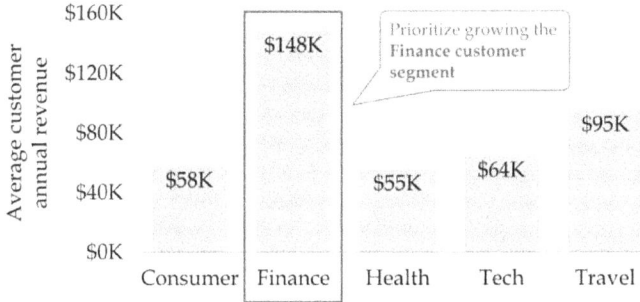

Existing customers in all industries are more valuable than new customers

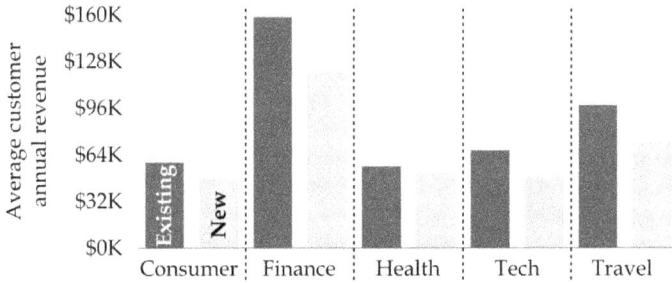

It is better to keep an existing customer than to acquire a new one

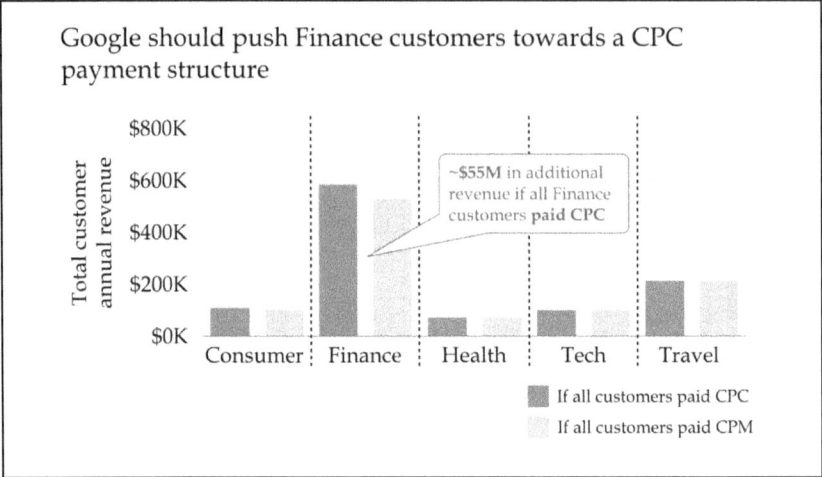

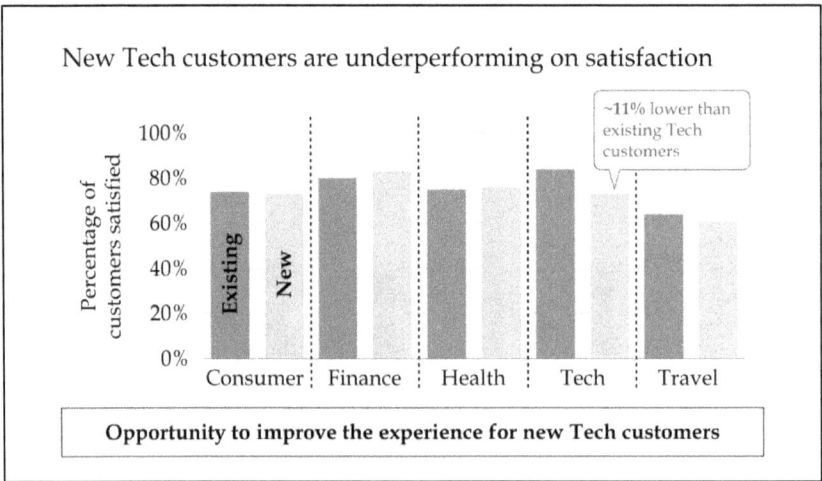

# Conclusion

## Summary

In this chapter, we'll go through a summary of everything we've covered.

**Conducting company research**

There are four different sources of information you should use:

1. 10-K Annual Report

2. Tech articles

3. Current and former employees

4. Analyst reports

A SWOT analysis is a helpful framework to develop a perspective.

**Behavioral & resume questions**

To answer behavioral and resume questions, prepare 6 – 8 different stories that draw upon your past professional and personal experiences. Have at least one story for each of the following themes:

- Leadership

- Teamwork

- Problem Solving

- Resilience

- Integrity

- Decision Making

- Communication

- Interpersonal Skills

When asked a behavioral question, mentally run through this list and select the story most relevant. Structure your answer using the STAR method.

Additionally, you should prepare for the "walk me through your resume" question. Start with a strong opening statement, highlight your most impressive experiences, and connect those to your interest and fit with the role.

**Motivational questions**

For motivational questions, there are three different questions you should prepare for:

1. Why do you want to work at this company?

2. Why are you interested in this role?

3. Why are you interested in tech?

If the company is truly your number one choice, make sure to state this. If the company has a strong mission or core value, ensure that you mention it in your answer.

## Case interviews

Case interviews are 30- to 45-minute exercises in which you and the interviewer work together to develop a recommendation to answer or solve a business problem.

A case interview can be broken down into seven steps:

- Understanding the case background information

- Asking clarifying questions

- Structuring a framework

- Starting the case

- Solving quantitative problems

- Answering qualitative questions

- Delivering a recommendation

Each step has strategies that you should use to solve the case efficiently and effectively.

## Mini-cases

Mini-cases ask for a plausible answer or solution to a business question or problem. They are different from case interviews in that they are shorter, more role-specific, and assess you more on the content of your answer.

Have at least a basic understanding of how to answer questions for all types of roles since tech roles are becoming increasingly cross-functional. You can never be sure what kinds of questions you could get asked.

These are the common types of questions for each role:

- Strategy & business operations

- o Company performance questions

- o Growth questions

- o Competition questions

- o Risks and threats questions

- o Trends questions

- Product management & marketing

  - o Product improvement and design questions

  - o Product marketing questions

- Business & corporate development

  - o Potential acquisition questions

  - o Valuation questions

  - o Potential partnership questions

- Operations

  - o Process improvement questions

  - o Pricing questions

  - o Forecasting and capacity planning questions

- Analytics

  - o Estimation questions

  - o Metrics questions

- Finance

- o Profitability questions

- o Budget questions

- o Finance and accounting questions

**Data challenges**

A data challenge is a take-home assignment in which the interviewer will give you a small dataset and a business question to answer. You will analyze and interpret the data and then make presentation slides to communicate your answer.

There are seven steps to complete a data challenge:

1. Understanding the objective

2. Becoming familiar with the data

3. Cleaning the data

4. Structuring a framework

5. Analyzing the data

6. Synthesizing the data

7. Making presentation slides

# Final Thoughts

Congratulations on making it through this book!

You now know exactly what to expect for interviews for business roles in tech. You know the types of questions interviewers will ask, what they are looking for, and what strategies to use.

The next step is to practice using all of the strategies and techniques you have learned. What separates candidates that get multiple job offers from those that don't get any is the amount of time invested.

Preparing for interviews takes a lot of time and effort, but the investment is worth it to land a fulfilling, high-paying job.

You have all of the information you need to succeed. The strategies in this book have already made you much more well-prepared compared to the average applicant. The rest of the work is up to you.

I wish you the best of luck!

## I'd Love to Hear From You

If you found this book helpful, I'd be incredibly grateful if you left a quick review on Amazon. It only takes about 30 seconds and it makes a huge difference in supporting me as an independent author.

**Click the link below to leave a review**:

https://www.amazon.com/review/create-review?asin=173333811X

**Or simply scan this QR code with your phone:**

I read every single review and yours would truly mean a lot.

# About the Author

Daniel Li is an experienced strategy consultant that has worked at Bain & Company, Airbnb, Johnson & Johnson Health Tech, and Capital One. He has worked with technology startups and Fortune 500 companies in e-commerce, software, hardware, and telecom.

Daniel holds a B.S. in biomedical engineering from Duke University and an M.B.A. from the Wharton School of the University of Pennsylvania.

www.ingramcontent.com/pod-product-compliance
Lightning Source LLC
Chambersburg PA
CBHW070308200326
41518CB00010B/1928